RONDA

BY

JOSE PAEZ CARRASCOSA

COLLABORATIONS

TRANSLATION BY: Mrs. Grace Rogers

PROLOGUE: D. Gonzalo Huesa

PICTURES: D. Salvador Ordóñez «Cuso»
D. Marcelino Pajares

DRAWINGS: D. Cayetano Arroyo

My sincere thanks
to everyone.
THE AUTHOR.

ISBN: 84-300-3885-X
DEPOSITO LEGAL: M. 15.884-1984
IMPRIME: RUAN, S. A. - Alcobendas (Madrid) - O. 92

DEDICATION

To all those rondeños
whom life separated from
their city and whose eyes
and hearts return always
to the abrupt beauties of
their beloved Ronda

PROLOGUE TO THE THIRD EDITION

The success which we foretold when this work made its first appearrance three years ago, is now with the third edition, a reality.

It has been so successful, because the pleasant dialogue, between the author and the reader was the right idea in this work. I think that every man that sits down to write, attempts to start a dialogue with his possible readers, in this way trying to escape his own incommunication.

I also believe that a man who takes a book in his hands always has a longing, never satisfied, to converse with the author about the many nuances in any work that can be ambiguous and incomprehensible.

José Páez has come through both these concerns and has offered us his vision of Ronda in the form of a pleasant conversation which starts as one starts reading and only finishes on closing the book on the last page.

This, I think, is the reason for his success. He has not overdone the conversation of erudite quotations or grandiloquent discussions. He has cherished the image which he has offered us of Ronda and very often he has allowed the reader or the visitor to the town to see and feel for himself the enchantment and witchery which the town casts over him.

He has wished this work to serve as a guide to visitors; but he has eschewed turning it into a habit. His simplicity and naturalness is what is so apreeable because the reader feels he is accompanied by a friend who speaks to him with the naturalness that we feel every afternoon when we stroll round the town.

Let the new reader judge for himself. The other readers, the ones of the two former editions have had the opportunity of corroborating this and this corroboration has made this new edition necessary.

There are towns over which we will never have said enough or written enough. Ronda is one of these. And José Páez has understood this.

G. Huesa Lope
Ronda, Christmas 1980

INTRODUCTION

I, sir, am from Ronda, queen and lady of the Serrania, protected by her monuntains and summits just like a spoilt child by God's will. Situated on a plateau at 780 metres in the south west of Malaga province, she watches over and protects us, being a natural and the most impregnable fortress in this part of Spain.

The most impregnable?

Don't you believe me? well then, come with me to our bridge and, from it you will realise the truth of what I am saying and also the beauty which up till now you have missed.

Look over there, where the sun is setting, can you see those blue peaks? Well, those are the Sierra de San Cristobal and the Sierra de Grazalema, the first thing that he, who comes from America by boat, sees. They rise to a height of 1,640 metres, and they have the highest rainfall of the whole peninsula.

But don't let your eyes stray; look to the left. That is the Sierra Perdiguera; that is where the road to Algeciras passes towards Gibraltar, that piece of Spain in the hands of...

What are you telling me? that you have never heard of the smugglers and bandits of Ronda? But, wherever have you been all this time? have you never heard of José María the 'Tempranillo' or the 'Pasos Largos'? Well listen. There are still people in Ronda who can tell you of the times that they have gone to a certain place and have returned loaded to Ronda and they could also tell you that to ride to Gibraltar on a horse was just a pleasant outing; with a good guide and getting up very early, it was a ten hour ride, and, after a light lunch an a rest in La Linea, the return trip and arrival at dawn in Ronda.

But do not linger. Come to the other side of the bridge where the sun is showing us its first rays. Have you never seen a sunrise or a sunset in Ronda? Pity! you don't know what you have lost! but don't worry that is easily remedied...

Look, those are the Sierras of Melequetin, Hidalga and the Sierra de las Nieves. That is the highest point in the province of Malaga, the Torreccilla, 1,910 metres high.

On clear days, from that point one can see the whole of the Costa del Sol.

In the Sierra de las Nieves there is a kind of tree called Pinzapo Abies, a botanical species exclusive only to this place and to the Urals, in Russia, although there are a few examples in the Sierra de Gredos, near Madrid.

You are right I have heard it said that it is a plant from the tertiary era.

Now look down. Well? wonderful don't you think?

Friend, there is nothing more beautiful than this Gorge with its river Guadalevin at the bottom.

What does Guadalevin mean?

It really means 'The deep river', though other versions translate it as 'Milk river'.

Has the river carved out the Gorge?

No, nothing like that. The Gorge has not been formed by the erosion of the river. Come here to the beginning of the bridge. You will see for yourself from here, how the formation of the gorge has come about; Look how the outlines of the rocks on the right hand

8

side fit into the hollows of those on the left hand side; yes, this was a seismic formation either through an earthquake or some other form of geological movement; though it is also true, and you can see it for yourself on the rocks, that the depth of the Gorge has been made greater and will continue becoming deeper due to the erosion from the water of the river.

There is quite a flow in the river which increases greatly when it rains for it has its source in the Sierra de las Nieves and near Ronda it picks up water from the streams la Toma and Las Culebras; further down the valley it joins the river Alcobacin and later continues its flow in the river Guadiaro.

In winter. It's quite frightening to pass over the bridge, isn't it?

I should think it is cold in winter and how! You are right, in winter it is cold and it snows on the mountains; but our climate is extremely healthy and, besides the winter is short. But, what do you think of the summer?

The summers are marvellous. Yes, it is hot some days in August; but when the sun sets the temperature is so agreeable that it makes one forget the few hours of heat which after all, is what one expects of summer.

In any case it is a dry heat and Ronda is about the most healthy place you could find: without any contamination or anything worrying and besides with springs and autumns that are the envy of many people.

And what does Ronda live on?

Ronda as the principal town of the Serrania is its commercial centre; it has a selection of shops that are as good in quality, in price as any that can be found in bigger towns.

It counts on the elaboration of pork products, its chorizo and hams being world famous.

The making of Castilian crafted furniture is very important, it is made in quality woods such as chestnut or walnut.

Today several factories have been started for the making of cheese from the rich goat's milk and ewe's milk of our serrania and also a few factories that turn out confectionery and tiles.

Finally, agriculture completes the list of its resources.

Tell me, why did you say that Ronda was an impregnable town?

Do not be too formal in Ronda everybody is a friend.

You will tell me whether it is impregnable or not.

On its northern side there is the gorge of 100 metres in height; on the park side it is 180 metres high: on the west the same characteristics apply and precipices which united to the ramparts continue to the Alcazaba to the south. There are the principal gates into Ronda; the Almocábar gate and the Charles I gate. The first one is from the XIIIth. century and gave access to the Alcazaba and the second built in the XVIth. century has the arms of the House of Austria over it.

These gates gave access to the Alcazaba of Ronda and were well fortified because this southern side is the only natural access to the city. Then on the eastern side double ramparts continue to the gates Exijara and Phillip V and then continue again to the Tajo.

What do you say about the fortifications of the city of Ronda? Was it really inaccessable?

A city like this will have a rich history won't it?

It has, and a great part of it has been planted in its ramparts and houses. But allow me first to give you a general outline. Then you will accompany me and see these features that history has written on the stones of the city.

A BRIEF HISTORY

The origins of the city of Ronda go back to the Bastulo Celts, who called it Arunda, although their lands had formerly been inhabited by prehistoric man; their megalithic monuments such as «Los Arenosos» and the cave of «La Pileta», with its paleolithic paintings and neolithic ceramics prove this.

Ronda had very few commercial ties with the Phoenicians because the latter on their arrival in our land, found near Arunda a village of Iberian origin called Acinipo. There they settled and improved the existing constructions. For them this was an ideal situation in view of their commercial aspirations with the interior of the country and because Acinipo is situated at the same distance from Malaga and Cadiz, both Phoenician colonies.

Later Arunda became a Greek colony, being called Runda.

And could you tell me what Arunda and Acinipo mean?

Well, Arunda means «Surrounded by Mountains», and Acinipo means «The Land of Wine».

In the second century B.C. the Romans entered the peninsula and expelled the Carthaginians. Immediately our town, taking advantage of its situation, is converted into a fortress in which the Castle of Laurel was built. Acinipo was converted into a town, becoming a municipality with powers to mint money and later on its citizens acquired the same rights as any citizen of Imperial Rome.

Sertorius, in his war against Pompey, destroyed Runda, and changed its name to Munda.

In the year 45 B.C. a pagan temple was built commemorating the victory of Caius Julius Ceasar over Cneus and Sextus the sons of Pompey. We will speak about this temple on our visit to Sta. Maria. So the Roman domination continues and the natives on their side assimilate their culture and customs.

With the invasion of the Sueves, the Vandals and the Alani and still later the Visigoths both Munda and Acinipo were destroyed and plundered. But the Gothic king Atanagildo begs the Bizantine Emperor Justinian for help against the Agili. The latter is rewarded with the south eastern coast of Spain which includes Ronda.

The Bizantine Greeks seek the lands where their ancestors had possessed Runda. They discovered the ruins of Acinipo and Runda and realised that the former were in better condition and also its situation pleased them more, so they installed themselves in it and they called it Runda.

For this reason Acinipo is called Ronda la Vieja (Old Ronda).

It is after the year 711 under Arab domination that Ronda takes up its place in the history of Spain, becoming one of the most important towns and fortresses in the south of Spain.

When our country was invaded the ruins of the castle of Laurel and the city of Munda were found. It was decided to build a town on these ruins which would be called Izna-Rand-Onda, the city of the castle, the chief point of communication and union of the Caliphate with the African territories.

Under the rule of Omeya, Ronda became the capital of a Waliato or Kura a province with the name of Takuruma, which comprised all of this mountainous region.

In this epoch important buildings were raised such as mosques, palaces etc:, the walls were strengthened as well as its defenses. In the south wall the main door was opened, called the door of Almocabar, and in the east wall that of Exijara, joining the old suburbs to the 'Medina' (market).

Umar-Ben-Hafsun was born in 854 near our town in the village of Parauta.

Of noble Gothic Christian origen he fomented unrest from 899 to 917 under the rule of the Omeyas.

Taking advantage of christian discontent on account of Moslem abuses, he placed himself at the head of a large mozarabic army rising in rebellion against the Moslem troops and maintaining dominion over large regions of the south of Spain.

He chose as his headquarters a place named Bobastro, situated between the valleys of Abdalagis, Ardales and Alora here in the province of Malaga.

The courage and fame of this man from Ronda became more and more well known, numerous volunteers, desiring liberty and independence for their lives, religion and lands joined him.

The war was continued for ten years by the descendants of Umar-Ben-Hafsun until they were defeated by the Caliph of Cordoba, who totally destroyed the work of Umar.

The attempts of Umar to obtain the independence of our land is praiseworthy as he had managed to dominate the whole of the province of Malaga; part of that of Cadiz with Algeciras, part of the provinces of Granada and Almeria, even advancing against the province of Cordoba and capturing the town of Cabra on his way towards the capital of the caliphate.

With the disappearance of the caliphate of Cordoba at the beginning of the 11th. century the kingdoms of the Taifas appear on the scene.

Ronda becomes, under the Berber dynasty of the Banu-Ifran the capital of one of them, ruled by Abu-Nur who governs in peace and prosperity for 39 years.

New villages are born in its 'Serrania' and its buildings and industry improve.

During this period the kingdom of Ronda is coveted both by the kings of Malaga and of Sevilla. The latter, Mothadir of Sevilla murders Abu-Nasir, son and successor of Abur-Nur, at a banquet. The king of Ronda being dead, Mothadir incorporates into the kingdom of Sevilla the kingdom of Inza-Rand and all its territories in the year 1059.

With the invasión of the Almoravides (warrimg tribes from the Atlas) the name of our town Izna-Rand is changed into that of Madinat Runda and continues to be ruled by them for 71 years until they are expelled by the Almohades.

During the domination of these Madinat Runda sometimes belongs to Africa and at others to the kingdom of Granada, changing allies and enemies with extraordinary facility, until finally the Almohades are defeated at the battle of Navas de Tolosa.

The chronicles of Castile narrate that during this epoch the moors of Ronda were the most intrepid and courageous in this land of the moors.

Alfonso XI relates how he destroyed lands, and vineyards in Ronda, Antequera and Archidona hoping to weaken his enemies through lack of food.

The king of Castile fought for four days in this campaign in our land but had to abandon it for lack of provisions.

In the year 1314 the king of Granada Ismail III frightened by the advance of the Christian forces under Alfonso XI seeks help from the African Benimerines, this is granted by the sultan of Morocco Abul Hassan, who sends his son Abomelic.

This latter having arrived declares himself King of Ronda, Algeciras and Gibraltar, making Ronda the capital of his dominions.

At this time prosperity and splendour comes to our town. There are important constructions such as the bridge in the old suburb or the stairs in the rock with 360 steps built into the live rock which supplied the town water from the bottom of the gorge.

Abomelic was killed in the battle Alberito by the troops of Alfonso XI, it is later incorporated into the kingdom of Granada.

In this epoch Ronda and its Serrania gain great importance in the history of the reconquest as she is coveted by everybody due to her situation on the frontier between the kingdoms conquered by the Christians and the Nazarite kingdom of Granada.

During the 15th. century Ronda comes down in the world due to the furious attacks from the christians.

In 1407 after the conquest of the village of Zahara, the infante Fernando sent his chief commander D. Ruiz Lopez Davilos with 2000 lancers in the hope of conquering Ronda.

But it was too strongly and well guarded with many defenders and winter was coming on.

The conquest of the city was not possible until the accession of the catholic kings to the throne of Aragon and Castile. They determine to finish once and for all with the Arab domination in Spain. Fernando the Catholic meticulously prepared the conquest of the Algarbe of Malaga to the west of the province. He succeeded totally in the campaign of 1485. with the conquest of Ronda on the 22nd. of May of the same year.

On the 15th. of April 1485 the king leaves Cordoba and marches towards Puente Genil and on the 19th. he has already positioned himself in Cartama, Coin and Benamaques.

Hamet el Zegri, gobernor of Ronda and head of the tribe of the same name leaves the city of Ronda in order to defend the villages besieged by Fernando the catholic.

Despite their courage and efforts Coin falls on April 27th. on the following day the same happens to Cartama.

After conquering the whole of the valley of Cartama the christian troops reach the gates of the city of Malaga, to where Hamet el Zegri manages to arrive with reenforcements and eventually save it.

On the 5th. of May the marques of Cadiz marches to conquer the city of Ronda accompanied by D. Pedro Enrique with 3000 horses and 8000 foot soldiers.

King Ferdinand marches towards Antequera and Archidona besieging the city of Loja in order to keep his troops from Malaga busy. At the same tpme he sends his artillery from Cartama and Coin to Teba where the whole army has to meet in order to conquer the city of Ronda and where the marques of Cadiz had arrived first.

All theses stratagems were necessary in order to conquer the impregnable city of Ronda.

On the 11th. of May the governor of Ronda, Hamet el Zegri heard that the true intention of the christian armies was not the conquest of Ronda but, by pretenting to besiege Ronda and Loja in order to distract his troops a second christian army would march to the final conquest of the city of Malaga which would logically be badly guarded.

The 12th. of May having arrived and Hamet el Zegri seeing the christian army camped round Ronda, did not doubt the news he had received. He prepared his army to march to the defense of Malaga, naming Abraham al Haqui, as governor in his absence.

The siege of the city of Ronda was ordered for the 13th.its total army consisted of 9000 horse and 20.000 soldiers leaving as rearguard 4000 horse and 5000 infantry soldiers more.

Hamet el Zegri's rage was immense when he realised on his way to Malaga that Ronda was blockaded. He decided to return with his whole army and tried to break the blockade, but in vain.

The attack of Ronda was ordered for the 14th.

The artillery was positioned at three points. The first pointing towards the octagonal tower of the castle: the second at the low walls round the gate of Almocabar and the third on the eastern side of the town from the heights of Tejares, which totally y dominated the town. It is noteworthy that in the conquest of Ronda lombards were used as an artillery instrument of war.

After a heavy siege of seven days and without water, for the Marques of Cadiz had cut off the supply to the town, a breach was opened in the octagonal tower which later crashed to the ground.

In the middle of the battle, ensign Alonso Yañez Fajaro with his sword in one hand and the standard in the other and after many efforts managed to place the standard on the ruins of the tower. This gave great encouragement to the christian troops in their struggle

and discouraged the moors who took refuge in the Alcazaba.

The governor, when he saw the desperate situation ran up the white flag, surrendering the city.

Hamet el Zegri after desperately trying to break the siege for ten days blinded by rage and courage returned with his men towards the city of Malaga in whose defense he died in 1487 not before cursing the defenders of the city of Ronda. calling them traitors and weeping for the loss of his beloved city.

King Fernando accepted a parley ordering the cessation of all hostilities and conceding their lives to the vanquished and only their furniture as property.

The christian captives crawled out of their dungeons and prisons half dead and extenuated. The majority of them had been taken prisoner in the battle of Axarquia, in number approximately 400. They were given food and clothing and sent to Cordoba, to be received by queen Isabel. After they were sent to places of their own choice. In order to commemorate this event queen Isabel ordered their chains to be hung before the church of San Juan of Toledo.

The greater part of the moslem population went to the mountain villages under christian government. Others went to Africa and the most important personalities went Alcala de Guadaira in the province of Sevilla, where they were given houses and properties.

The standards of the catholic church, the crusades and of the king of Castile were placed on the keep of the caetle and on the 24th. of May king Fernando V of Aragon enteredhthe city of Ronda in triumph.

The old mosque was converted and consecrated to the christian cult under the patronage of Santa Maria de la Encarnacion and to whom queen Isabel had a great devotion.

A solemn Te Deum was sung there and returning to the ruins of the octagonal tower king Fernando orderd a church under the patronage of the Holy Spirit to be built, for the conquest that year coincided with Whisuntide.

Wishing to join the queen who was waiting impatiently in Cordoba, he marched there entering in triumph, having left the count of Ribadeo, D. Pedro de Villandrado as governor of Ronda.

After the conquest of Ronda a distribution of lands to the nobles and knights who had participated in the conquest of the town was made. On the 25th. day of July 1485 in Cordoba, the town was given the faculty of governing itself by the same laws and jurisdiction which the towns of Sevilla and Toledo possessed.

Ronda was converted to the lordship of prince D. Juan, son of the catholic kings who married Margaret of Austria, and who on his death retained the overlordship of the city.

In 1499 the princess went to Flanders and then began the irregularities in the honourable administration of the city, taxes on food products, which came into the city were considerably augmented. Under these circunstances the purveyors decided to remain on the outskirts of the city and start small markets, which were the origins of quarters called 'el Mercadillo' and 'San Francisco'

In time the 'San Francisco' quarter became the agricultural quarter and the «Mercadillo» continued to grow to its present size built on the north side of the Tajo.

Due to the morisco uprising in our Serrania and in the Sierra of Granada because they had not totally submitted to the capitulation agreed to at the conquest of Granada between king Boabdil and king D. Fernando, Ronda became the centre for expeditionary forces which attempted to subject the rebels; but after the reverse suffered by D. Alonso de Aguilar, the Gran Capitan's brother, at the hands of the moriscos and things being in a bad state, the catholic kings came to Ronda and stayed at a palace today known as Mondragon palace.

From then on the Serrania was sometimes at peace and at other times threatened by the Moriscos, until finally in 1609, by a royal decree, of Phillip III, the latter were finally expelled from Spain.

Many years later, it is interesting to note, that Ronda heroically opposed the French invasion, for its mountain people do not allow themselves to be dominated very easily.

Nonetheless on the 10th. of February 1810 Joseph Bonaparte entered Ronda, lodging in the house of the marques of Moctezuma.

During the time the French remained in Ronda there were numerous acts of resistance by the people of Ronda who attempted

to throw out the invadors. Finally they succeeded when a man from the montains shot the French general Boussain on the outskirts of Ronda.

When the invadors left our city they destroyed the old Arab Alcazar (Fortress) and many other artistic monuments of great value.

◀ *Minaret of San Sebastián*

Bandoleros

Sto. Domingo Convent ▶

New Bridge

◀ *Arab Bridge and Romain Bridge*

THE VISIT

And now that you know a little of our history we will begin our visit from here.

This is la Plaza de España. In it you can see the building with arches and an arcade, that was the Town Hall. It dates from 1843, but perhaps you would like to know that now the Town Hall is in the old military barracks on the old Town Square.

In the centre of the square there is a bust of D. Antonio Rios Rosas, a famous «Rondeño» who became a minister and president of the congress in 1862. He was distinguished by his honesty and eloquence. The other buildings, as you see, match the central building of the square.

Well, let's go along Villanueva Street, on the right here. Here you can see some houses built in the style of the XVIIIth. century, with the classical grills and windows of Ronda.

We will now turn to the right along Coronel Corrales Street and enter Mina Street.

*House
of the Counts
of Santa Pola*

New Bridge

Guadalevín river

The Mercadillo ▶

We will go into **the gardens**.

Come here, to the right, so that you can see the gorge in all its splendour, and the bridge from its foundation up.

This is the **New Bridge**, «The Bridge of Ronda». And I call it this, as the whole world calls it so, because really this symbolises the town in all its aspects.

Contemplate this masterpiece, spanning the gorge at its deepest, but also narrowest. This is really impressive, rousing pleasure and fear at the same time.

It was built by D. Antonio Martin Aldehuela, an Arogonese architect from the village of Manzanera in the province of Teruel.

He began this work in the year 1751 on the foundations of another bridge.

He was helped by master builders from this town, among whom D. Antonio Diaz Machuca is worth mentioning, His machinery, invented by him for this task, was admired by all the engineers who came to see the construction.

What do you mean machinery created by this master?

Well, this man who was a Rondeño invented several machines and apparatus with which, and with the help of 3 or 4 men, sufficient material could be lowered in a day which would employ 200 men for a week.

The work was finished in the year 1793, which means that it took 42 years to build. It is 98 metres high and is built entirely of blocks of stone.

It rises on its foundations from the depth of the gorge. It is formed at its base of a small arch, upon which is raised a central arch (which has a great room above it) and two smaller lateral arches.

In the central room of the bridge there is today a restaurant, but formerly it was used as a prison, the entrance was through that lpttle square building on the right, which was the guard tower.

Look from here, you can see perfectly both from the left and the

Convent of Madre de Dios ▶

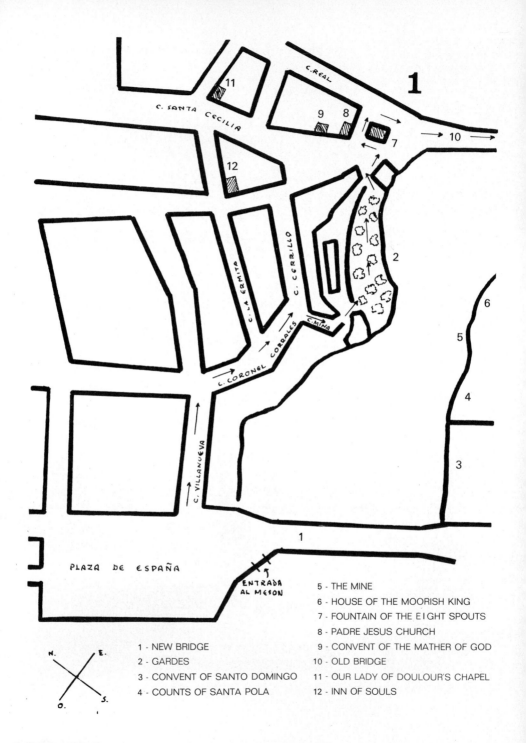

1

C. REAL

C. SANTA CECILIA

11

9 8

12

7 10

C. LA ERMITA

C. CERRILLO

C. CORONEL CORRALES

C. MINA

2

6

5

4

3

C. VILLANUEVA

1

PLAZA DE ESPAÑA

ENTRADA AL MESON

N. E. O. S.

1 - NEW BRIDGE
2 - GARDES
3 - CONVENT OF SANTO DOMINGO
4 - COUNTS OF SANTA POLA

5 - THE MINE
6 - HOUSE OF THE MOORISH KING
7 - FOUNTAIN OF THE EIGHT SPOUTS
8 - PADRE JESUS CHURCH
9 - CONVENT OF THE MATHER OF GOD
10 - OLD BRIDGE
11 - OUR LADY OF DOULOUR'S CHAPEL
12 - INN OF SOULS

◀ *Philip V Gate*

right of the bridge the remains of the foundations and columns of the former bridge.

It was built 1735 and consisted of only one arch. It stood for only five years.

I have heard that the architect of this bridge committed suicide in order never to have to build another such in his life?

Look, this is a very romantic story and there are several variations, but the truth is that. D. Antonio Martin Adelhuela died in Malaga, where his remains lie in a parish of that town.

Look, behind us there is a plaque which Ronda dedicates to its sister town Cuenca. Those houses built on the very edge of the precipice we call 'The Hanging Houses of the Tajo'.

Ronda has, due to its situation, a great similarity to the city of Cuenca.

And what is that old building opposite us?

That is the **Convent of Santo Domingo**, the Catholic kings ordered it to be built. When it was finished it was handed over to the patronage of the Dominican friars. Of the original building only the church is left but no worship is celebrated there now. It is used by the Rondeño furniture cooperative, the pride of Rondan craftsmanship, their furniture recalls the famous quality and workmanship which the craftsmen of Ronda so richly deserve. Its entrance is on the so called slope of Santo Domingo at the end of the brigde on the left. It has three naves, and an elavated half orange shape, with a beautiful panelled cieling, in the Mudejar style with a choir.

The inquisition was held in this convent.

We must also mention that in this church there is a mausoleum with the remains of D. Jose de Moctezuma y Rojas and those of his wife.

He had it built in his life time and at his expense and it occupies the site of the former chapel del Rosario.

What beautiful houses can be seen from here?

House of the Moorish King ▶

You are right, it is the north eastern part of the city, and from these terraces the over all view is marvellous.

These terraces are of recent construction, they were built by the Town Hall, bent on beautifying and bettering the city. From them the contemplation and stonework of the Tajo and the city has been enhanced, and also the peerless view of the bridge and the remains of the convent of Santo Domingo and the house of Los Guerreros Escalantes, today known as the **House of the Counts of Santa Pola**.

Which one? The one with the Arab windows and arches?

As you can see it is a manor house with many Arab remains. It was built on the remains of an Arab shrine, as a matter of fact it was the tomb of an Arab noted for his life and for his virtues, what we would call a good man.

On the portal we can see a large heraldic coat of arms of the Guerreros de Escalantes.

But let us continue down. Look from this corner at the view of the **Old Bridge** and of the gorge.

This bridge has been at times called Arabic and even Roman.

It consists of only one arch, 10 metres in diameter and 31 metres above the level of the river and it is 30 metres long and 5 metres wide.

Until the end of the last century there was an inscription on it which. D. Jose Moreti has transmitted to us and which I am going to reproduce.

It goes thus:

> Ronda rebuilt this construction under its joint corregidor with Marbella, D. Juan Antonio Torubio de Quiñones for the king our lord in the year 1616.

What do you think of the view that we enjoy from here?

Beautiful, but tell me, what is that aristocratic ochre coloured house?

It is called the **House of the Moorish King.**

Ah! that is the house with the remains of the entrance of the sultanas baths, built by the Arabs.

Listen, now we are going to abandon flowery speeches, romanticism and legends and we will go to the truth.

This building was not constructed for a sultana's baths, nor for any thing like that, for the only thing that this does is to increase our fantasy and lead us away from the truth.

The Mine or shaft constructed by Abomelic around the beginning of the XIV century as a military edifice. Ronda in the XIV century, being the capital of the kingdom of the Benimerines in this part of Spain which also included Gibraltar, was the most important natural fortress in the whole of the southern part of the peninsula.

The stairs were built in the live rock, partly protected by bricks and adobe, with a few hollows and windows in order to let in the light, and a few rooms or extensions used as dungeons where the prisoners slept. The whole staircase is vaulted and built in sections, One can deduce from this visit that it really was of military origin.

In times of sieges, fights and civil wars the Arabs used to form a human chain of christian slaves, drawing up water from the depth of the river into the interior of the town. The said stairway is well camouflaged and on its inside walls can be seen the marks and signs made by the slaves that worked there.

There is a proverb about the stairway that says:

In Ronda you will die heaving up water skins.

During the reconquest of Ronda it was discovered by the Marquis of Cadiz and it was guarded so that no-one should escape that way.

But tell me: during droughts or blockades of the river it was impossible to get water out of it. What was the use of this shaft?

Look, opposite the access door there is a fountain which still supplies Ronda today and formerly the water ran down the river towards the entrance door to the shaft in the depth of the Tajo. well, this stairway is at the back door of the so called 'House of the Moorish King' axactly opposite the spring.

This 'House of the Moorish King' is a misnomer. The historian Hernan del Pulgar tells us about the shaft when he describes the conquest of Ronda and our compatriot Vicente Espinel in his Life of Marcos de Obregon's squire refers to it as one of the most important remains from Arab domination in Spain. But the house, except possibly a few Arab vestiges in its gardens, dates from the beginning of the XVIII century and was restored at the beginning of this century.

Its facade has some tiles representing a moorish king, perhaps Abomelic, in a hieratic position. Its balconies are Ronda forged, with some Sevillan tiles, all from the beginning of this century as I have said.

Now this house is as well known in the world as is the Tajo or the bridge. People from all over the world are interested in it and this fame is due to Dña Trinidad Schultz, Duchess of Parcent.

This lady of great beauty and intelligence bought the house from Mr. Perrin of Baltimore, U.S.A. at the beginning of the century.

She enriched it with the best furniture, paintings, ceramics and decorations which she brought from all over the world. She had the most important families of that epoch visit it and gave Ronda fame both on account of her house and because she encouraged local arts to surge up again.

But a certain section of Ronda did not agree with her ideas and she suffered some persecution. The last straw was a coffin with her initials on, which appeared on the square named after her, in the garden laid out with her money. This action made her decide to sell the house. To Alexander Machinley, the American President's grandson and she left Ronda with a heavy heart.

This lady, whose family originated from Malaga married D. Manuel de Iturbe, called viceroy of Mexico, because of his immense fortune. Their daughter Dña. Piedad Iturbe married Prince Hohenlohe, Kaiser William II cousin, they are the parents of D. Alfonso Hohenlohe.

After, the duchess married the duke of Parcent and after his death became the dowager duchess of Parcent.

But let us continue, time does not pass in vain. We are now in Mine Street whose paving is a reproduction of the old Ronda style.

What a beautiful square.

This is where the **Mercadillo** begins.

The mercadillo?

Yes Sir, for us this is the modern town, built on the north side of the Tajo, the Mercadillo.

And why?

Listen, its beginnings are really very interesting and I am going to tell you about them, so that you can see that in this town even the names and simple things are history.

When Dña. Margaret of Austria, widow of D. Juan left Ronda to return to Flanders in 1499, the administration and government of Ronda suffered great changes. The excises and taxes which were demanded at the gates of Ronda dissuaded the sellers from bringing all sorts of articles. These latter instead of bringing their products to the usual places, left them on the plain at the doors of the town, at the principal gate Almocabar or in the Ejido zone, the gate at the bridge.

The repeated attempts of the authorities to stop these abuses proved useless, in fact, they were the origin of commerce and the fairs which have been so important to Ronda.

To the south of the city, opposite the principal gate, that of Almocabar, on the flat ground by the entrance, there was a hermitage to the Visitation. Around it there were about a hundred stalls or little shops where the traders began to lodge in order to save on the taxes for entrance into the city.

Because of their wish to emulate, the traders situated at the Ejido by the bridge, in other words, where we now are, also erected a chapel, today called **Padre Jesus.** This image and that of our Lade of Doluours attract great devotion in the town of Ronda.

The facada is gothic, even though one can see renaissance influences in the bell tower, having been reformed several times, the last, the actual building in 1755.

Sta. Marie.
Altar
of the Sagrario

Sta. Marie.
Altar of our Lady
of Dolours

The church is not very large but it is well distributed, divided into three naves separated by two brick columns, and two other columns on either side with capitels bordered with flowers in relief. These colunms support the central nave which has a beautiful coffered cieling.

Notable people of Ronda were baptised in this church, such as Vicente Espinel a man of letters, and Rios Rosas a politician or the bullfighter Cayetano Ordoñez «Niño de la Palma».

The square and the Calle Real (Royal Street) was until the middle of the last century the commercial centre of Ronda. The **Fountain of Eight Spouts,** which was the public fountain for the inhabitants of that district. It is a simple fountain with eight spouts, from which it derives its name, with a big trough at the back to water the animals.

It is not known when it was built, but traces in its structure shows it to have been built or restored in the time of Charles III. It is the most typical fountain with dash in Ronda; it has the town coat of arms with the yoke and arrows.

Near the church of Padre Jesus is the **Convent of The Mother Of God,** Which is one of the most beautiful corners of Ronda.

It is built in the Mudejar Gothic style recently restored and converted into a national school for girls. In this convent which dates from the middle of the XVI century there has been preserved its church with a baroque altar in gilt and its principal courtyard.

Ascending to the first floor one can see a bautiful arch in mosaics and brick work which leads into the library.

From here, if you do not mind, we will return to the **Old Bridge** from where we will continue our visit, and allow me to show you the third bridge.

That bridge which you see down there at the entrance to the gorge, is the smallest and is the **Arab Bridge**, even though everybody calls it the **Roman bridge.**

It was built during the Arab domination in the century XIV, it has been damaged by the rise and fall of the Guadalvin river and has had to be totally restored.

It is small and seems unimportant, but I would like you to know that it was the principal entrance into Ronda through the old quarter, near the Exijara gate, recently discovered and restored and the remains of which you can see over there in the walls.

What are those ruins in the background, behind the bridge?

Those are the **Arab Baths**.

The building was the property of the duchess of Parcent, afterwards sold to Sr. Zini Vito, one of the pioneers for tourism in Ronda. It was he, who discovered, perhaps by chance, the remains of the baths which we are now going to see.

These were discovered, as I said, by Sr. Zini Vito, when a farm which was built on top of them, collapsed, when they were inmediately rediscovered because they were completely covered by sand, stones and other objects due to the swelling of the river.

When the 'Direccion de Bellas Artes' (Conservation Ministry) saw the importance of the said buildings they indemnified the said gentleman for all his work and efforts and took over the work tehemselves.

These baths are among the better preserved and interesting in the whole of Spain, even though they have lost their marbles, gypsium and mosaics with which the Arabs used to cover their buildings.

They were built approximately at the end of the XIII and beginning of the XIV century.

The baths consist of three rooms whose structures show for what they were used.

In the first one can be seen, very well restored by the Direccion General de Bellas Artes, the chimney for the outlet of smoke and hot air and the remains of a stove to heat the water that came from the draw well along channels. In this room can still be seen the channels along which the hot air passed to the central chamber.

This second chamber is divided into thee naves covered with vaulting sustained on brick horseshoe arches. A few of these arches and their capitals have been restored; but there are some

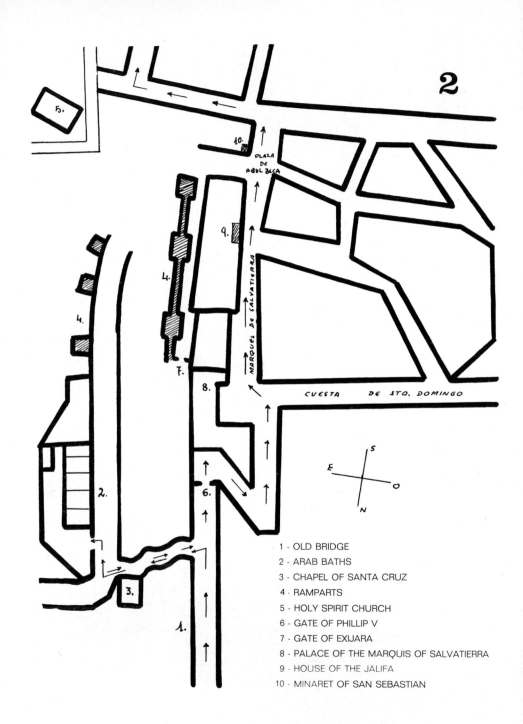

2

1 - OLD BRIDGE

2 - ARAB BATHS

3 - CHAPEL OF SANTA CRUZ

4 - RAMPARTS

5 - HOLY SPIRIT CHURCH

6 - GATE OF PHILLIP V

7 - GATE OF EXIJARA

8 - PALACE OF THE MARQUIS OF SALVATIERRA

9 - HOUSE OF THE JALIFA

10 - MINARET OF SAN SEBASTIAN

other very interesting ones, for example, a Roman capital very eroded by time, of great value which together with the lateral domes oblige one to stop and contemplate this chamber carefully.

From this room we will pass to the third which was the room in which everybody relaxed and was massaged.

Passing through a recently discoverd door we come into a water deposit or fountain without its original covering of bricks. It is very well preserved and could have been used as a place for ablutions before entering the principal building.

These baths were surrounded by various buildings and industries, the archaeological value augments day by day, as work on the excavation continues.

Do you like it? Look up and see our restored walls and the gate of **Exijara:**

It is the gate about which I spoke before, but you can see it better from the draw well, it is that higher building, on the corner.

Arab towns were triply fortified, as is this town. Ronda was fortified with three walls or ramparts whose remains you can see perfectly from down here and which gives one a great feeling of strengh.

The first of these ramparts starts from those towers that you see continuing from the baths; from the second start the principal ones, and above them the fortified houses were like a third rampart. Between the remains of the first and second ramparts was the old quarter and the Jewish quarter. This quarter gradually disappeared after the conquest of Ronda by the Catholic Kings because the Jews and mudejares who lodged there were in the habit of helping their coreligionists who had taken refuge in the mountains, making it very easy for them to penetrate the town by night in order to plunder and obtain provisions.

What is that building that looks like a chapel or a hermitage?

That is the chapel of **Santa Cruz.** In this hermitage, the owners, masters and workers in the leather factories, potteries and other trades which have disappeared, worshipped. Latterly it has been restored by the Direccion General de Arquitectura.

Well now let's go up the hill and rest at the gate of **Phillip V.**

Here on the right you have a plaque saying that this gate was built during the reign of Phillip V. in the year 1742.

It has been proved that when the old bridge was built in the year 1616 there was a gate called Bridge gate until in the year 1742, on receiving its present structure the name was changed to that of Phillip V.

Let us continue up and enjoy this ascent for its pleasantness and the beauty of its streets and houses.

Here we have the **Palace of the Marquis of Salvatierra.**

It was built at the end of the XVIIIth. century and the actual structure date from that time. It was built on the site of some Arab houses, and it belongs to the marquises of Salvatierra and de Parada who live in it at varioua times of the year.

The building is of great artistic and historic value in the interior, but as it is a private residence, entrance is not permitted. It has a magnificent façade in the renaissance style with double corinthian columns on each side with some suns on its doorhead. Above this there is a beautiful Ronda forged balcony, it is made with forged and sculptured iron.

On the upper part of the façade can be seen the figures of four Peruvian Inca Indians which reveal a colonial influence. Their postures are very simple for the first is a young girl who is timidly trying to hide her nakedness, and the second is a naughty boy who is putting his tongue out in a gesture of mockery. The figures on the other side represent the same characteristics.

Above all this in the centre is the family coat of arms.

If you like we will continue up the Salvatierra Street.

Yes, whatever you say.

Look at theses interesting and picturesque streets.

Are the majority of these houses being restored?

Yes, but all under the direction of the General de Arquitectura, so that they neither break up nor lose the structure of this quarter.

Look at this house to the left, with its two coats of arms.

It is the **House of the Jalifa.**

Of the Jalfaifa?

Yes, it was here that the last Jalifa of Tetuan, when Morrocco was a Spanish protectorate educated his children and maintained his family.

Well the hill is finished and we will rest for a few minutes in this square called **Abul-Beca,** in memory of a famous Arab poet born in Ronda.

Here we have the **Minaret of San Sebastian** so called because the mosque that occupied the site until the conquest of Ronda was converted into a church under the patronage of San Sebastian.

Of the said mosque and church only the tower of the minaret remains. Built in the XIVth. century by the Nazarites it has been recently restored, notice a few ornamental remains and mudejar constuctions.

In the lower part you can notice a beautiful horse shoe arch and the interlacing bricks, and a few ceramic remains that originally decorated the whole tower.

Let us go along Armiñan Street and turning to the right we get to the **Duchess of Parcent's square.**

This is the original military square of Ronda. It is one of the most charicteristic squares of the city. The place where jousting and tournaments were carried on, today its centre is a garden, and there is a bust of the Ronda writer Vicente Espinel a poet and musician besides being a censor and critic of books. He was a friend of Lope de Vega and of Miguel de Cervantes, frequently having long chats with the latter when he was in Ronda and when D. Miguel de Cervantes lodged in the Posada de las Animas (The Inn of Souls), today it is an old age pensioner's home. Vicente de Espinel's musical side is unknown to many people; but he was a good musician who added the fifth string to the Spanish guitar.

On this square from left to right we have first the **Church of Charity** from the XVIth. century. founded by the Rondeño Pedro de

Miranda in order to serve as a place of burial for the condemned and unknown persons, Today it is occupied by the sisters of the Cross.

Round the corner from this building there existed a poor house for poor passers through, to lodge in.

More to the left, is the church and convent of **Santa Isabel de los Angeles**, the Clare nuns, it was built in the middle of the XVIth. century.

Opposite the cathedral, on the other side of the gardens, stood the **Castle of Laurel** under Roman domination, converted into an Arab fortress.

On the 26th. of August 1812, it was dynamited by the French when they left Ronda; thinking that they would return they calculated that in this way they would encounter no resistance once all the missiles, powder and bombs stored there to be used by the Spaniards in their defence, had been destroyed.

As you will remember Ronda as a natural fortress was very well protected by the hand of God who defended it with ravines and gorges; but it had, and has a natural access just behind the ruins of the castle of Laurel. This is where its principal door was to be found, the gate of Almocabar. A second that gave access to the Alcazaba, was the gate of Images which also disappeared in the said explosion.

From the southern part of the city can be seen, and even better from the slope of the Images, the remains of the ramparts and towers, which are today called the Castle.

It is a school run by the Salesians, the foundation Moctezuma, because the marquise of Moctezuma promised and brought to Ronda Augustins and Salesians. Initially the Salesians occupied the manor house of the marquis, today called Santa Teresa. When the Augustins left they took over the direction of the Castle.

Continuing with the buildings in the square we find the **Old Military Barracks.**

This building was constructed in 1651, as you can read on the

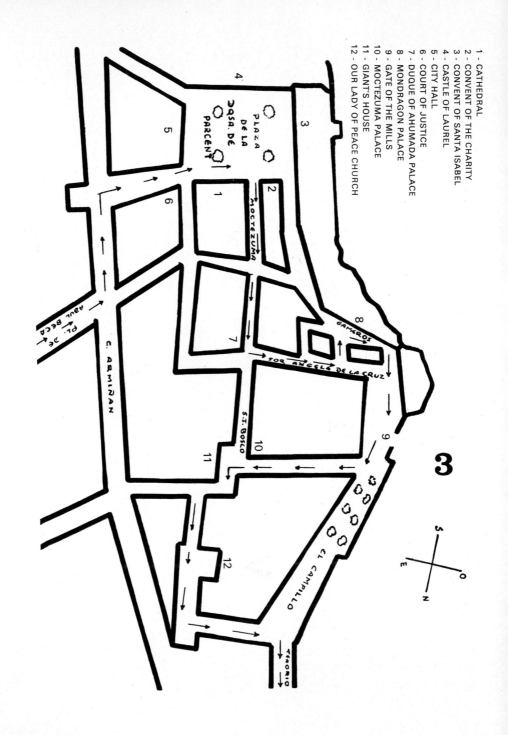

1 - CATHEDRAL
2 - CONVENT OF THE CHARITY
3 - CONVENT OF SANTA ISABEL
4 - CASTLE OF LAUREL
5 - CITY HALL
6 - COURT OF JUSTICE
7 - DUQUE OF AHUMADA PALACE
8 - MONDRAGON PALACE
9 - GATE OF THE MILLS
10 - MOCTEZUMA PALACE
11 - GIANT'S HOUSE
12 - OUR LADY OF PEACE CHURCH

PLAZA DE LA CASA DE PARCENT

MOCTEZUMA

PL. DE AZUL BECA

C. ARMIÑAN

GAMEROS

SOR ANGELA DE LA CRUZ

S.T. BOSCO

EL CAMPILLO

TENORIO

3

N S E O

inscription recently discoverd on the façade; it was restored in 1734 and again in 1818. It was at this time when its original entrance was changed and the building suffered a great transformation.

The back of this building which gives onto the Armiñan Street, has one of the oldest stores which are conserved in Ronda. It was the old public granery and in the lower part were the old silos for the grain.

Today it is being restored by the Direccion General de Arquitectura for the New Town Hall. Every attempt is being made to preserve the original beauty of the building, adding others, such as a coffered Mudejar cieling of the XVIth. century, donated by the countess of Santa Pola, a direct hieress of the Guerreros de Escalantes, no better place could have been chosen for its preservation than the dome in the entrance to the future Town Hall.

Tell me, on its façade is the coat of arms of Ronda but the one on the left, from where is it?

The one on the left is from the town of Cuenca, sister town of Ronda, an agreement come to in the year 1975.

The white building with the coat of arms of the catholic kings on its façade is today the **Court of justice.**

This is the building where Margaret of Austria, lady of this principality and wife to D. Juan, son of the catholic kings, heir to the throne lived. He did not live to occupy it as he died when he was a student at Salamanca.

This building has had different uses since Dña. Margaret left for her native Flanders, ending up as a court of justice today.

Listen, regarding this, I would like to explain something to you that perhaps you do not know. So you can rest a little, because truly you have not stopped talking.

Do you know since when the colour black has been a sign of mourning and sorrow for the loss of a dear one in families in Spain?

Well no, I don't know really.

The catholic kings felt such sadness and sorrow at the loss of their son D. Juan that they changed the national tradition of white for mourning into black.

Very interesting, thank you.

Well, now we have in front of us one of the most important monuments of the city.

Santa Maria la Mayor is beautiful both inside and outside, it is interesting and mysterious at the same time.

The façade itself tells us about the building, of its history and its beauty. Different from the façades of churches and cathedrals to which we are accustomed, the tower, which you can see from every part of the city, tells us of its charecteristics and design, of all the alterations and constructions which this building has suffered in its time. A mudejar tower built on the foundations of a minaret it is topped with a beautiful renaissance belfry.

On the right side there is a lovely long balcony built in the reign of Phillip III, they were to be the boxes, from which the nobles and authorities of the city of Ronda could watch the jousts, bullfights and other public acts.

Entering through the little tower door, to the right, we pass through a room where the remains of the Mirhab arch of the mosque can be found, adorned with inscriptions and arabesques from the Nazarite dynasty and which reminds us of the oratory of the Alhambra at Granada.

This mosque was built at the end of the XIIIth. century and the beginning of the XIVth.

Let us go in and we shall see that the building is bigger than we had expected from the outside.

Built in the highest part of the city, we are told that in this very same place there had been a temple erected to the memory of Julius Ceasar, of which nothing remains except perhaps, some possible remains of the foundations and a plaque which until recently historians referred to, and on which one can read IVLIO DIVO MUNIPES to commemorate the victory of Julius Ceasar over Pompey's sons, Cneus and Sextus at the battle of Munda in the year 45 B. C.

Those same walls would be used for the later construction of the principal mosque and then later still for the principal church of Ronda.

The mosque was converted into a church devoted to Sta. Maria de la Encarnación, to whom Isabel was very devoted.

King Ferdinand granted it the category of Abbey. It had honours and devotions which are stipulated for cathedrals and its chapter was allowed to nominate pariyh priests for Ronda, Arriate, Cuevas del Becerro and Serrato until the concordat of 1851 in which the size of the greater parish was reduced.

The building itself is in two very different architectural styles.

The part to the south is late gothic from the end of the XVth. century with on its right side renaissance influence because of the restoration it had undergone after an earthquake befell this city in 1580 and which damaged its most important buildings.

Here we have the beautiful baroque high altar from the end of the XVIIIth. century, with numerous vegetable decorative motifs, salmonic columns, fretwork etc:, gilt and polychromed on its lower parts. It has the images of the Immaculate Conception and St. Ann with the infant Virgin. On the left there is a churrigueresque altar also from the end of the XVIII th. century, a reliquary altar it has an Our Lady of Doulours attributed to Roldana.

To the right of the high altar there is a fresco of St. Cristopher painted by a painter from Ronda called Jose de Ramos in 1798, which reminds us of the great paintings of this saint in the Spanish cathedrals of Seville, Toledo etc:.

In the centre is the choir, which cuts it in two.

The choir is by unknown builders. It was finished in 1736 in the plateresque style, the lower choir stalls are of walnut with biblical motifs and the rest in cedar wood with very good carvings of saints and apostles.

Only one of the organ cases, built in 1710 in this church remain.

In the centre there is a walnut lectern by local carvers, with 4 of the books of gregorian chant that still exist in the church today.

These are XVIIth. century choir books, of parchment illuminated and in polychrome of great artistic merit and value.

On the pendentives of the domes in this part of the church can be seen, recently restored, motifs of the Loreto litany.

After the earthquake of 1580, in which the northern and western part of the church was destroyed, it was decided to enlarge it.

A church was built a replica of Granada Cathedral in renaissance style, with corinthian and tuscan columns. This construction took from 1584 to 1704.

This part of the church consists of three naves. In the centre there is a great dome with 4 medallions which represent the 4 evangelists. It is sustained by 4 great columns, two in corinthian style with large cornices and the other two in Tuscan style. There are 4 large entrance doors. The high altar was built in 1727 by Estaban de Salas the presbitery. The next year the pulpit in carrara marble was built.

I have to explain that the high altar of Esteban de Salas was destroyed in 1936. To fill this noticibly empty space in the church the lateral altar of the Sacred Heart of Jesus has taken its place today.

This altar, which was formerly a secondary one, is carved in red pine and attracts every visitor's attention for its magnificence.

It is in the form af a little temple, executed at the end of the XVIIIth. century in red pine by unknown artists, although it is attributed to some monks. It is interesting to notice some of its fretted details which give a unique personality to this magnificent work.

To the right of this altar is the sacristy with the remains of the church treasure, another eighthgregorian chant choir books, XVIIth. and XVIIIth. century chasubles, a marble changing tóble for the priests and a few documents referring to church matters.

Well , after our visit what do you say if we stop a little and have a little something in the «Sotanillo», parochial centre of Sta. Maria? And so we can have a little chat with the sacristan D. Vicente Becerra, a good man who has lived here for the last 50 years, and he has a good local wine and pleasant conversation and where better than in the parochial centre that he runs.

Fine.

If we take the street immediately to the right ox the cathedral we come imto the Moctezuma street. We shall come across many manorial houses in this part of the city, with their heraldic coat of arms which tell us about the history of these families.

For example, this one to the right is the house of the dukes of Ahumado, founder of the Civil Guard, or this other one to the left which belongs to the Hinojoso Bohorquez family, a house with one of the most beautiful patios in the city of Ronda.

We will continue along the Sor Angela de la Cruz street and we will come to the **Mondragon Palace.**

Among all these white houses there is one aristocratic one in stone, which is why it is commonly called the «Stone House». It is clearly an exponent of the cultures, styles and civilizations through which Ronda's civil architecture speaks to us.

This building which was originally built by Abomelic, king of Ronda at the beginning of the XIVth. century (1314) has been the seat of kings and governors. From there Hamet el Zegri governed this province under the Nazarite domination.

Of that period there only remain the foundations and a few subterranean passages which run from the garden of the house to the old fortress of Ronda. In its walls one can see perfectly the changes and restorations that have taken place over the years. There are two mudejar style towers and an aristocratic renaissance style portal, with stone horse steps to assist horse mounting, a door into the stables and a mudejar style coffered ceiling in cedar wood which reminds us of the Spanish Golden century.

In its interior, in the old part there is what is called the arab patio, which in reality is mudejar and which clearly shows the restorations which have taken place in the palace.

Arab arches over renaissance decoration, restored old arab mosaics with mosaics of the XVIth. century.

It was over restored at the end of the XVIth. century by Melchor de Mondragon. Ascending to the first floor there is besides a large dome with family escutcheons a large chamber with a mudejar coffered ceiling, the best in the palace.

The house was inhabited on two occasions by the catholic kings. The first time by D. Fernando in 1485 on the occasion of the conquest of Ronda and later by Isabel and Fernando in 1501 on account of the rebellion of the moriscos.

Later it passed into the hands of D. Fernando de Valenzuela, marquis of Villasierra a favourite of Mariana of Austria, widow of Phillip IV. D. Fernando de Valenzuela fell into disgrace and was deported to Mexico dying there miserably.

We will leave Mondragon and go to the **Plaza del Campillo, formely Puerta de los Molinos,** and from its balcomies we can see the old road that takes us to the city ramparts and its gate, today called the Gate of Christ. This was the access gate from the mills at the bottom of the Tajo into the town. From hege we can see the gorge in its entirety and at its deepest with the handle of the cauldron at the very bottom and a beautiful view of the Mercadillo.

Let us return along Jose M.ª Holgado street and in the little square of San Juan Bosco we have on our right an old manor house with the coat of arms of the Moctezuma and Rojas family. This is the house built by D. Jose Moctezuma y Rojas, grandson in a direct line on the masculine side of the great emperor and king of Mexico, his tomb is to be found in the church of Santo Domingo.

Opposite is the **Casa del Gigante** (the Giant's House), the name was given to it by the people of the town because on its façade there is an effigy of a Punic Hercules found in the house and whose ciclopean shape gives it the aspect of a giant.

This house, which was built in the XIVth. century, is an example of a middle class arabic house.

In its interior it has a central patio with an old well surrounded by columns, and two chambers where one can see the remains of decorative Moorish plaster work on their walls, arches and spandrels, which remind us again of the Alhambra of Granada, which was built during the nazarite period in Granada.

It has suffered different types of restoration because it has been put to different uses, such as for Mayor Ruiz Gutierrez de Escalante and later even as a home for abandoned children.

Let us continue down San Juan de Letran street and we shall get to the square of the Beato Fray Diego Jose de Cadiz.

In this square is the house where the Beato Fray Diego Jose de Cadiz died, on the 24th. of may 1801, and the **church of La Virgen de la Paz.**

This church is devoted to the cult of the patron saint of Ronda, one of the oldest statues of thz city of Ronda, to whom cult was rendered in the XVIth. century in the hermitage of San Juan de Letran, which has now disappeared.

The tradition of this statue goes back to the time of Alfonso XI but the actual statue seems more likely to be from the end of the XVIIth. century.

The temple possesses one nave only and several altars from the end of the XVIIIth. century.

It has a churrigueresque altar with an artistic shrine with mural paintings where the patron saint and mayoress of Ronda in perpetuity Our Lady of Peace stands.

At the feet of our Lady is a silver casket containing the remains of the Blessed Fray Diego.

In this church there is also a statue of Cristo de la Sangre which is venerated, it is by the famous statue maker from Sevilla Duke Cornejo, a pupil of Martinez Montañes, and a statue of Ecce-Homo of the school of Granada.

We will lreturn to Armiñan street and back to the New Bridge, we shall cross the gorge and go over to the Plaza de España and on to the bull ring. If you remember, here we began the tour.

Here, my friend, we shall have to stop before going in, to explain to you not about the building but to let you know that you are entering the **Ronda Bull Ring,** the sanvtuary of bull fighting on foot.

If our eyes as catholics look towards St. Peter's of Rome, and if the mohamedans look towards Mecca, the eyes of devotees of bull fighting look towards this place.

So, please look at its entrance, baroque, the exact opposite of the style of our schools of bullfighting which is classical and without any baroque, others may indulge in that.

It has tuscan columns supporting a broken pediment with the royal arms in the centre and a balcony of iron forged in Ronda with taurine motifs.

We shall enter so that you may see the bull fighter's cathedral of the world.

Before anything else I must say that our bull ring belongs to the Real Maestranza de Caballeria (the Royal Institute of Knights) the chief 'Real Maestranza' of Spain, anterior to that of Sevilla, Granada, Valencia and Zaragoza.

It was founded by order of Phillip II in the year 1572, though its origins go back to the time of the catholic kings.

This order was charged with the military education of the nobility, both as to horse riding and the use of arms, always having in view maintaining the activity of its members who in case of need should be ready to set out for any place in which they might be needed.

The deeds and battles of our 'Real Maestranza' since its foundation are innumerable.

But let us drop the 'Real Maestranza' who built this construction for their particular use rather than for bull fighting entertainments as we understand them today. well, as you know, before this building was erected the members used to have their bull entertainments and festivities on the parade ground, as I explained to you when we were visiting the old city.

The ring was inaugurated in may 1784. It is the widest ring in the world with a diameter of 66 metres and it is the only one that has a stone parapet. The exit for the bulls, the presidents's box and the royal box are situated on the same side the ring, besides it is the only one that is totally covered.

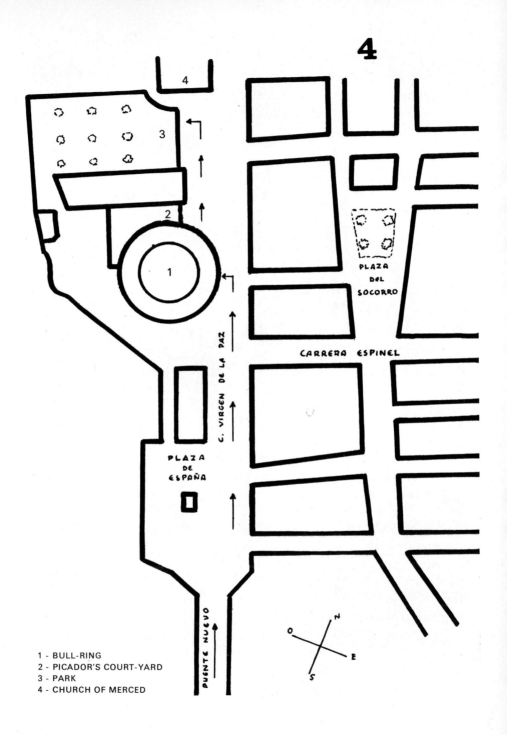

4

PLAZA DEL SOCORRO

CARRERA ESPINEL

C. VIRGEN DE LA PAZ

PLAZA DE ESPAÑA

PUENTE NUEVO

1 - BULL-RING
2 - PICADOR'S COURT-YARD
3 - PARK
4 - CHURCH OF MERCED

N
O
E
S

It has 176 columns and nearly 5.000 seats.

The traditional 'Goyesca' bull fight takes place there and lovers of bullfighting from all over the world come to learn what Ronda bullfighting is and to watch the art of bullfighting from our master Antonio Ordoñez.

This bull fight is enacted in memory of Pedro Romero, who according to the chroniches fixed and gave life to the golden rules of modern bullfighting.

Do you know that Pedro Romero was the master whom history relates killed 6.000 bulls.

But, doesn't that seem a lot of bulls to you?

My friend, don't you know that besides killing 6.000 bulls he killed the 6.000 face to face.

He was born in Ronda in 1755 and entered on the life of bulls at eight years old. He left it at 72 and died at 90 without once having been wounded by the horn of a bull.

He was a director of the Sevilla school and founder of the Ronda one.

I told you that he entered on the life of a bull fighter at 8; I should have said that he was born a bull fighter.

Listen, and see if I am not right.

His grandfather D. Francisco Romero, began as is known, and as was the custom of his time: The bravest men used to stand in front of the bull, hat in hand, or a cape, but merely as a pastime. The bullfighting of that time, to call it something, was performed by knights on horse back, in other words spearing and wounding the valiant beast on horse back. He became so expert at it that he began to teach it, the use of the cape and how to kill under the rules he had acquired from his own experience and he invented the red cloth in order to kill the bull face to face placing before lovers of the sport the bull fighter's crew.

His father, Juan Romero was the one who organised the cuadrilla, (the bull fighter's crew) with picadors, banderilleros, etc.: and he died at 102 years old.

And he, now you know all that he did! as if Pedro Romero had never heard bulls mentioned in his home!

On going out, the arch and gateway joined to the ring is the picadors entrance to the ring. It has the Spanish royal coat of arms the same as on the principal door.

This picador's courtyard was used as a yard for comedies before the Espinel theatre, now demolished, was built.

Now we will go to the **Alameda or Park.**

To the right we have the **Iglesia de la Merced** Carmelite convent founded by the Mercedarian ogder in the XVIth. century. Today it is occupied by H. H. Carmelites, who in their daily tasks produce typical local confectionary, for those who may require some, such as Ronda cakes or excellent home made bread.

Let us go into the **Alameda** which is the most important garden in Ronda.

It was laid out on the Ejido esplanade of the Mercadillo, in front of the convent de la Merced and finished in 1806.

Not one centime of municipal rates was spent on its outlay, for the work was paid for by the fines exacted from those who had either been obscene or provoked scandal on the streets.

The author of this ingenious and humourous idea was the then mayor of the town at that time, D. Vicente Cano.

The Alameda had several interesting things on the promenade by the Tajo, such as a series of busts of the whole royal family of Spain. At the entrance there were some inscriptions which I here reproduce for their curiosity and which no longer exist. They were removed during the Republic. D. Jose Moreti copied them and they go like this.

To the discreet town.

I have dedicated my enthusiasm to you
And the money I have spent,
So that this project may last
Depends on your care.

70

To the malicious Town.

Oh! don't be surprised at my tears
On seeing your lack of patriotism
And your innate selfishness
When you criticise this work.

To the Ignorant Town.

Of you foolish river,
Who unable to criticise
I only heard you murmur
What a pity about the money!

And another who said
It's finished
And it hurt no-one
For no-one was asked for money
For the cost
Fell on those poor people
Afflicted by their calamities
And who were rescued at public expense.

Now if you like we can go to the end of the park to look on the deepest part of the Tajo which on this side has a depth of 185 metres.

Do you know what this central balcony is called? It is the exclamation balcony, because everyone who comes here utters the most typical exclamation from his part of the world.

What is the most typical one here in Ronda?

It is C...

That building that you see on the side of the hill is the **Sanctuary de la Virgen de la Cabeza.** It consists of an hermitage where the Virgen de la Cabeza is venerated and of some caves, where some hermits called the lonely ones lived during the XVIIIth. century.

The brotherhood of la Virgen de la Cabeza used to bring their virgin in a procession to Ronda during a very popular pilgrimage, which unfortunately has now disappeared.

It is a very interesting place to go to because, apart from visiting the sanctuary there is a wonderful panoramic view of Ronda which is really fascinating.

Now that we are in the Alameda I want to show you a Pinsapo, for although we have seen several during our visit, because we generally have them in our squares, here there is a good example.

As I said before the Pinsapar is in the Sierra de las Nieves. In case on your return, you wish to see it, you turn off at km. 12 on the San Pedro road at the sign post Rajete, you go along it until you get to a farm called 'La Nava' and from there you can walk and see them. There you will find some very interesting examples and perhaps if you climb to the top of the Sierra de la Nieve to the summit of the Torrecilla which is at 2.910 metres, you may be able to see from Malaga to Gibraltar, that is to say the whole of the Costa del Sol and besides perhaps a cabra hispanica jumping about on the heights.

On your way out of Ronda I would like you to stop in the **San Francisco** quarter.

It will be very easy to recognise this sector because once you pass the ramparts all the white houses that you will see on your left and your right will be different from the rest of Ronda. You will now be in the San Francisco quarter.

I spoke of it before when I was explaining the origens of the Mercadillo.

It was born as a small market, when the traders at the end of the XVth. century refused to enter the city of Ronda in order to avoid paying the taxes and excises with which to swell the municipal coffers.

Some inns and taverns were built for traders and passers through and so a new quarter began which later would become the agricultural quarter, for the majority of traders decided to abandon the principal entrance to Ronda and to locate themselves to the north at the exit of bridge gate, today called Phillip V.

From the esplanade you can see the principal gate into Ronda. **Puerta de Almocabar** and the walls that separate the San Francisco quarter into two parts: the part that was built inside the ramparts and that on the outside, about whose beginnings I have spoken.

La Puerta de Almocábar (the cemetary gate) led to the Alcazaba and to the city, though there was a second door, which has now disappeared the gate of the Statues of which we spoke when we were visiting the parade ground.

This gate built in the XIIIth. century, consists of three doorways, with horse shoe arches between two semicircular towers which may have been sentry towers. On these towers there are some round stones in the form of crosses which were used during the conquest of Ronda in 1485. To the left there is another doorway, from the XVIth. century, built in the time of Charles I.

In the background you can see the remains of the **Alcazaba,** where the Salesian school now is and to the right is the **Iglesia del Espiritu Santo** (the church of the Holy Spirit).

This church was built on the orders of Fernando the catholic on the ruins of an Almohade octogonal tower which defended this natural access to the city and was destroyed by the christian lombards during the battle for the conquest of the city.

It was consecrated under the appellation of the Holy Spirit, because Ronda was conquered on the 20th. of may 1485, a day which in that year coincided with Whitsuntide.

It can easily be seen that it was built in time of war: it is sober and austere like a military fortress. It was finished in 1505 the year queen Isabel died.

It consists of one nave with a large pulpit, in keeping with that time in which the preacher could be easily seen and heard.

The nave is 30 metres long and 9 wide. It has great simplicity and the style is similar to Isabeline Gothic covered by later alterations. The baroque high altar occupies the central apse with a painting above of the coming of the Holy Spirit and in the centre a painting on wood of 'La Virgen de la Antigua' in a beautiful bizantine style.

On the high altar there are three coats of arms worked in stone, the central one has the imperial eagle of the house of Austria.

The belfry was built later as well as the door which was enlarged, and above which there is a niche with the Holy Spirit in the form of a dove.

On the present esplanade before the Puerta de Almocabar we can see the **Capilla de Nuestra Señora de Gracia** (Chapel of our lady of Grace). the patroness of the royal order of the knights.

It was the fiirst temple on the new site in Ronda and it was built in the centre of the esplanade with the name Iglesia de la Visitacion. Later it was moved to the position it occupies today and named Virgen de Gracia.

As we are here it would be interesting to visit **The Convent of San Francisco,** on the outskirts of this quarter of the same name, it was founded by the catholic kings to commemorate the place monarch Fernando camped during the siege of Ronda.

Damaged during the war of Independence, it still preserves a beautiful portal in the isabeline style.

From the said French domination there remains an emplacement erected by the French and which is used by the Ronda regiment in garrison. It is situated on the north side and is Called 'The Fortress'.

The French govenor of the town had it built, placing several canons and mortar pieces facing the town of Ronda in it and threatening to discharge them if the bands from the sierra did not stop harassing the French garrison in Ronda. Together with the mountaineers the citizens of Ronda used to attack the soldiers of the French garrison at night, making their lives impossible.

So innumerable are the beauties of the city of Ronda as are innumerable the names of her illustrious citizens through the centuries who have carried with them the name of their beloved city through the whole world, some famous in the world of letters and others in arms.

To list their names would be interminable and you would not remember them, so if you will allow I will just refer to a few of them.

5

1 - ALMOCABAR GATE
2 - CHARLES I GATE
3 - HOLY SPIRIT CHURCH
4 - FORTRESS
5 - CHAPEL OF OUR LADY OF GRACE
6 - CONVENT OF SAN FRANCISCO

Church of the Holy Spirit ▶

Don Vicente Espinel, an illustrious Ronda, writer, author of the picaresque novel «Vida del Escudero Marcos de Obregon», The life of Squire Marcos Obregon», he was also an outstanding poet, creator of the Decima (a ten verse stanza), which is now called 'Espinela', he was one of the best musicians of Spain at the end of the XVIth. century.

He introduced the fifth string into the Spanish guitar, the so called prima, which gave the guitar a more popular character.

Don Antonio de los Rios y Rosas, an illustrious tribune and honoured politician.

He became a deputy, Minister and President of the congress in 1862, and ambassador to the Holy See. He declined other important positions and titles and those which he did fill he did so with dignity and honour, combating with great eloquence from the rostrum those whom he thought were not guiding the affairs of the government well.

D. Francisco Giner de los Rios (1839-1915), nephew of D. Antonio de los Rios y Rosas, can be considered as the master of liberal and lay intellectualism and he was the creator of the Institution of free Education.

Valle-Inclan, Azorin, Baroja, Antonio and Manuel Machado, Juan Ramon Jimenez, Ortega y Gasset, Perez de Ayala, Marañon, Azaña, Garcia Lorca, Dali, Buñuel, Guillen and others were influenced under his Institutions.

D. Fernando de los Rios (1879-1949), nephew and pupil of D. Francisco Giner de los Rios, was minister of Education, of Justice and minister of State during the Republic and embassador to the U.S.A. during the Civil war.

Joaquin Peinado (1898-1975), can be considered as the best painter born in this city.

He became a teacher in the College of Art in Malaga, later leaving for France where with his geniality in painting he became outstanding in the parisian school of painting.

He was an intimate friend of Picasso.

And what can you tell me about those Rondans that have triumphed in the art of bullfighting?

Listen, those gentlemen have not only triumphed: they have brought glory to the festival, founding a school in the difficult art of good bullfighting. Because, what do you think of the dynasty of the Romeros who gave life to bullfighting on foot? Or the dynasty of the Ordoñez, who have shown all over the world what real bullfighting is?

We will not continue as the discussion would become interminable. In letters, arts, politics and in folklore and in practically every cultural manifestation, Ronda counts on a great number of men whose fame is the logical complement which the greatness of man sets against the greatness of nature created by the fantastic situation of this city.

Besides that, my friend, I must tell you that I have not shown you all that there is to see in my beloved town. In order to do that we should need much more time and you say you have no more time.

But you must return and complete this visit the same as if it were an incomplete dream.

I could enumerate so many memories, odd corners and places that we have not been able to see or still have to see, that the list would be interminable; but when you do return you will have to visit the little temple of Our Lady of Dolours.

Built in the time of Ferdinand VI about the year 1734, It is situated in the place where the condemned to death were executed and where finally they said their last prayers before passing over to a better life.

Barroque, with an image of Our Lady of Dolours and some crown caots of arms in stone. Its columns are formed of stone figures also, they represent the hanged ones with their disfigured and fiendish semblances and their deformed faces and bodies.

Not very far from there you have the 'Posada de las Animas' the Ghost Inn, today a home for old age pensioners; though it has been restored it goes back 1500. The origin of its peculiar name comes from the entrance door where some shin bones and skeletons are depicted, which simbolise the end of this life, there is also a picture of Our Lady fetching some souls from purgatory. This old Inn was for drovers as well as for gentlemen (knights) who were passing through. It had the honour of welcoming the great writer D. Miguel de Cervantes y Saavedra, as well as many other important figures from all over Spain. There stayed a no less illustrious a person than the Rondan writer D. Vicente Espinel.

Dear friend, you are pursuading me to postpone muy departure.

No Sir, I am only trying to convince you of what has been left untapped.

I see, but I realise that you have only spoken to me of famous sons, monuments, and illustrious deeds, so, what about the ordinary people? and Rondan women?

How right you are, but you are in such a hurry!

The ordinary people, they are the begettors of all this splendour that is Ronda. As for the Rondan women I am sorry that I have not spoken of them before.

In general the Rondan woman is virtuous, religious and abounding in good qualities and was always at the side of her menfolk during the time of transcendental happenings in our town. In answer to your two questions, I tell you that the ordinary people also produced women that, through one circumstance or another are heralded in the deeds of our history.

Have you heard speak of 'Carmen of Ronda' that legendary woman on whom Bizet based his opera 'Carmen'.

During the war of Independence that woman, who was not very well thought of by the townsfolk, because they did not know quite what she did, had a great influence on the resistance to the French occupation on account of her movements and deeds. She was the one who gave warning of the dinamiting of the Alcazaba by the French, and thanks to her, it was possible to save part of it, as well as avoiding greater ills to the inhabitants of the town.

But let us continue with the ordinary people and talk about a woman whom everybody remembers with great affection. Ana Amaya Molina 'Aniya the Gypsy'; she was born in Ronda on the 27th. of September 1855, a 'great singer and dancer' (in the Andalusian style) it was said that when Aniya sang and played, the world came to an end. She was the grand aunt of the extraordinary 'artiste' Carmen Amaya who learnt many Rondan songs from her. She sang and played all over Spain, in the most reknowned places and with the best singers of that time. The queen Vitoria Eugenia made her a gift of a 'manton de Manila', after having performed at an intimate gathering for the royal family.

Loved and respected by everyne she was acquainted with artists and poets from García Lorca to Manuel de Falla, the name of Aniya the gypsy was on all their lips as a key figure of famous songs and songs from the Serranía.

But others of course, were to blame for deeds that were not quite praiseworthy, because of course, all sorts ingabit the Lord's vineyard.

Listen I am going to tell you the story of a Rondan man, a little legendary, whose wife was the cause of his ending his life outsede the law. This man was José Ulloa, a member of the team of Pedro Romero (the bullfighter) very skilled in the Rondan art of bullfighting. This man was married to a gypsy from Ronda, she was called Nena, also a dancer, he was delirious about her. One day when the war of Independence was over a bullfight was organised in Málaga, it was to celebrate the arrival of Ferdinand VII 'The desired one' back to Spain, and his services were required as second swordsman. Near the little town of El Burgo he fell from his horse, breaking an arm. Realising that there was no point in continuing he decided to return to Ronda. Arriving there rather late at night, he noticed that his wife was a little nervous and restless. Our friend became suspicious and began to search the house until he found, in a huge oil jar, the sexton of the neighbouring parish. He killed them both and fled to the Sierra.

Not long afterwards he appeared as a member af the famous gang 'The seven youngsters of Ecija' and even though this gang

*Sta. Marie.
Gothic Naves*

*Sta. Marie.
Renaissance
Naves*

Sta. Marie.
Arch of the Mirhab

Sta. Marie. ▶
Little house
of the Tower

was eventually brought to justice, Tragabuches remained in the Sierra until in time he disappeared without leaving a trace.

What he did leave behind him was a little rime, which has always been sung by the people of the Sierra and goes like this: 'A woman was the cause of my downfall, there is no perdition of man that doesn't originate from a woman'.

'Tell me, referring to Bandoleros, there must be many stories referring to them?

Many and interesting that would give you a clearer idea of the situation in our Serranía at that time and above all of the character of our Serrano people.

But friend, as you are in a hurry and you intend to return, because everyone returns to Ronda, I promise to tell you about them and continue to enjoy your company.

You must use your afternoon in seeing **Acinipo** and the **Caves de la Pileta.**

In order to visit them both you must go along the Sevilla road. At about 5 km. from Ronda you will find a crossroads which will take you to **Acinipo (Ronda la Vieja);** but if you continue on the Sevilla road to about 12 kms. to the left you will see a sign to the **Cueva de la Pileta.**

The road to Ronda la Vieja will take you to Acinipo; if you continue it will take you to the wonderful village of Setenil de las Bodegas.

Acinipo is situated at about 800 metres above sea level, in the heart of Roman Andalucia. Pliny and Ptolomy placed it in the celtic region Beturia, it became a municipality with right for minting money until it was destroyed by the vandals in 429.

Time has been much more generous than the vandals for it has proudly preserved the ruins of its theatre.

When you arrive you can admire, from the road the stage wall built with big stones. Much nearer and viewing it from the stone seats you will see that it has three doors and above them niches for placing either statues of gods or of tribunes.

Recently the rooms used by the actors have been discovered and also the place for the musicians, the stage and the space between the stage and the auditorium. Here you can see the remains of large red marble flagstones which covered the floor of the theatre.

Also the seating has been uncovered. You can see that the majority of them are worked in stone, as in Greek theatres, using the uneveness of the ground some stairways give access to the upper and lower seating.

The panoramic views are wonderful and around the theatre you will still see the remains of stones and tiles and the remains of houses and hildings which will help you to understand the barberous state of destruction to which the town was subject.

Some vertical stones will show even today the original limits of the town.

Finally return to the Sevilla road and follow it until you see the sign which will leave you at the very door of the **Cueva de la Pileta.**

You will go through such picturesque villages that they will look more like white spots in the Serrania (mountains). These villages are Montejaque and Benaojan, of Arab origen, hardworking, pretty, clean, friendly and proud of their land as nowhere else in Spain.

If you should stop in either of them you can visit one of the many factories which turn out pork products of well merited fame from our Serrania. You will also see how well the inhabitants look after their villages and keep them clean like the true gems that they are.

We have in our Serrania numerous caves of extraordinary value from the spelaeological and historic point of view. Besides the Cueva de la Pileta, we should also mention one called **Cueva del Gato** (the Cat's Cave) near the raiway station of Benoaján-Montejaque, which even today has not been totally discovered and where just recently a Valencian spelaeologist lost his life.

◀ *Bull Ring
entrance*

Interior ▶
Bull Ring

◀ *Tipical street*

The Arcs ▶

The Cueva de la Pileta was discovered in 1905 by D. Jose Bullon Lobato. Later in 1911 it was visited by the English colonel Mr. Vernet who through several publications in the English press, made it known to the world. Following on this, two experts Mr. Breuil and Mr. Obermaier studied and spoke of its prehistoric value.

It was declared an national monument in 1924. When you see it you will feel the immense pleasure of the beauty of nature harmonising so well with beauty created by man who lived here for thousands of years.

Traversing majestic chambers or narrow passages and galleries you will find wonderful shapes formed by nature and matching the stalactites and stalagmites. You will finds chambers such as the Bat's chamber, that of the serpents, the castle, the Moorish queen, the cathedral, the dead woman, the fish, the waterfall, the great abyss, the organ, the sanctuary, etc.:

Numerous ceramic remains and utensils from Paleolithic and Neolithic times have been found, some can be seen in the cave; others are in museums in different parts of Spain. You will see the skeleton of a young woman that in the course of time has become petrified.

You can also admire rupestral paintings of incalculable value in ochre, yellow or black; some of these in red or yellow dating from 24.000 years ago.

There are numerous signs and diagrams which are clearly magical-religious.

After walking for miles in the interior of the cave, you will re-emerge, contemplate the landscape which surrounds you and you will think; How wise is nature and how great the hand of God who concentrated so much beauty in so few kilometres of our Serrania.

Here, Sir, our visit is finished. Good day and good journey.

◀ *Pot's Handle*

Chapel of our ▶
Lady of Dolours

◀ *Almocábar Gate*

Gate of La Real ▶
Maestranza

Bullfighters

AVE MARIA

Vicente Espinel

◀ *Palace of the Marquis de Salvatierra*

◀ *City hall*

Old Bridge ▶

◀ *Mondragón Palace*

Holy Spirit ▶
Church

Pedro Romero

EPILOGUE

On writing this guide book, which I must say caused me some doubts and vacillations, I have not pretended to go into the profundities of the history and character of our beloved city; but rather, through my primal profession as a tourist guide in it, have I tried to impart knowledge of the monuments of our city, in which the places and monuments are being restored and more and more are being discovered every day augmenting the whole.

And I have tried, above all, to facilitate though perhaps lightly, her fundamental features.

To some this book will absolutely not satisfy them. To others it may serve as an introduction for later studies on Ronda. No essay and still less this one, is perfect or complete.

It will be enough for me if all those who read or use it will feel and live, as I feel and live the spectacle of a city which has known how to harmonise the beautiful grandeur of her situation with the beautiful grandeur of her urban planning to produce the charm of a unique Ronda. City of dreams, Enchanted city. The dreamed of city.

The author.

▲ *To awake up of Ronda ...*

Monument ▶
to Reiner M.ª Rilke

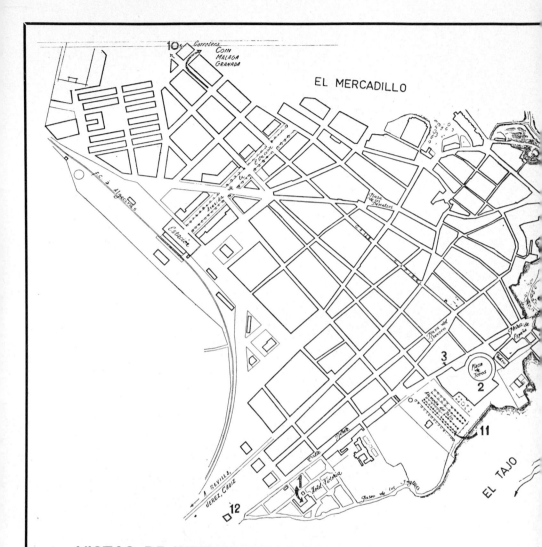

EL MERCADILLO

EL TAJO

VISTAS DE INTERES EN LA PLAZA

1.—Hotel Reina Victoria
2.—Bull-Ring
3.—Post office
4. Telephone
5.—Neu bridge and old prison
6.—House of the Moorish King

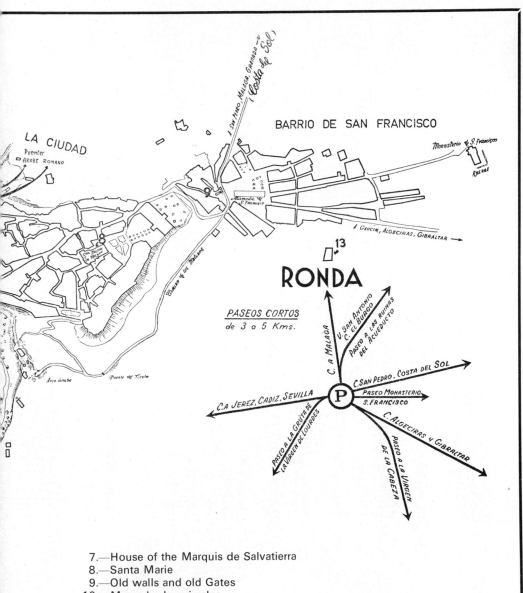

7.—House of the Marquis de Salvatierra
8.—Santa Marie
9.—Old walls and old Gates
10.—Mercado de animales
11.—Gardens
12.—Virgen de Lourdes
13.—Virgen de la Cabeza

Tipical street ▶

INDEX

◄ *Aniya la Gitana*
Pintura de Miguel Martín

◀ Gate of San
Francisco

Sta. Marie ▶
square

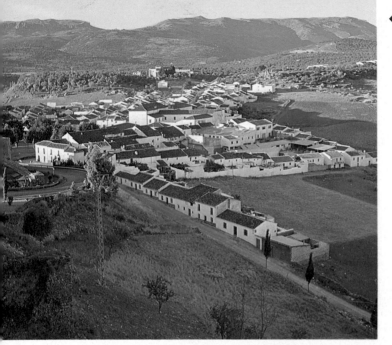

◀ *San Francisco*

Houses
on the Tajo ▶

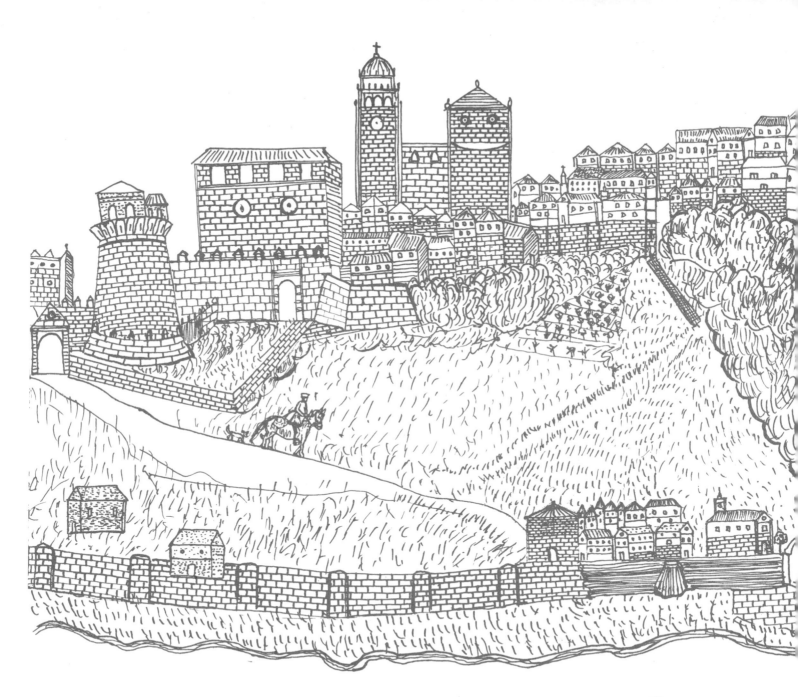

Ciudad de

Illustration from 1649
Followed by the
Counts of Santa Pola

Ronda

Ronda en 1.649
recopilado por Arrjo.

FOUR MORE SHERLOCK HOLMES PLAYS

by MICHAEL & MOLLIE HARDWICK

from stories by
Sir Arthur Conan Doyle

JOHN MURRAY Albemarle Street London

The four plays in this volume have been recorded in exactly corresponding text on two long-playing records (nos. DCO 1212 and 1213). They are produced by Michael and Mollie Hardwick and acted by Robert Hardy as Holmes, Nigel Stock as Watson and casts of well-known radio artists. These may be ordered through record dealers or direct from Discourses Limited, 34 High Street, Royal Tunbridge Wells, Kent. Two other records, uniform with these (nos. DCO 1210 and 1211), are also available, comprising versions of the stories *The Speckled Band*, *The Blue Carbuncle* and *Charles Augustus Milverton*, which, together with *The Mazarin Stone*, comprise the companion volume, *Four Sherlock Holmes Plays*.

Printed in Great Britain by
Cox & Wyman Ltd, London, Fakenham and Reading

0 7195 2839 9

FOREWORD

This volume has two predecessors – *Four Sherlock Holmes Plays* (1964) and *The Game's Afoot* (1969), both published by John Murray. Each contains four Sherlock Holmes plays specially dramatized for simple staging or for reading in class; and both, we may happily say, are widely used for both those purposes.

The present work is different. The four plays it contains are exact transcripts of four of the dramatizations included in our series of long-playing gramophone records of the Sherlock Holmes adventures, starring Robert Hardy as Holmes and Nigel Stock as Watson, supported by casts of well-known BBC players, and published by Discourses Ltd, 34 High Street, Tunbridge Wells, Kent. At the time of this book's preparation there are four such records in existence DCO 1210 (*The Speckled Band* and *The Blue Carbuncle*), DCO 1211 (*Charles Augustus Milverton* and *Black Peter*), DCO 1212 (*The Norwood Builder* and *The Disappearance of Lady Frances Carfax*), and DCO 1213 (*Shoscombe Old Place* and *The Illustrious Client*). The four latter plays are the ones included in this book.

Since the publication of the first two volumes we have had increasing evidence of the wish of educational bodies – especially ones in other countries or concerned with the teaching of English to foreign residents in Britain – to find recordings of first-class material linked to precise texts. It is yet another tribute to the qualities of the Sherlock Holmes stories of Sir Arthur Conan Doyle that these have been the subject of many such enquiries; and, rather than produce another volume of acting versions, we have decided to concentrate this time upon a word-for-word link between sound and print.

In their own right, these plays are suitable for dramatic reading in the classroom, but we venture to suggest that, considered alongside the recordings (which, by the way, are also available in tape or cassette form) they have much to teach English-speaking pupils about acting technique and foreign students about the use of the English language. That, at any rate, is our intention and hope.

MICHAEL & MOLLIE HARDWICK

CONTENTS

The authors wish to express their gratitude to
Baskervilles Investments Limited

THE NORWOOD BUILDER

Characters in order of appearance

SHERLOCK HOLMES

DR. WATSON

JOHN HECTOR MCFARLANE: an asthmatic young
lawyer.

INSPECTOR LESTRADE: of Scotland Yard. In his
forties and unrefined; lean and 'rat-faced' in
appearance.

JONAS OLDACRE: an elderly builder; shrewd but
uneducated.

MRS. MCFARLANE: John Hector's elderly widowed
mother, of quite ordinary origins.

TWO POLICE CONSTABLES

THE NORWOOD BUILDER

SCENE ONE

> [*221B Baker Street.* HOLMES *and* WATSON *are sitting by the parlour fire one morning*]

HOLMES: From the point of view of the criminal expert, London has become a singularly uninteresting city lately, Watson.

WATSON [*chuckles*]: I can hardly think many decent citizens agree with you, Holmes.

HOLMES: Ah, well, I mustn't be selfish, I suppose. The community is certainly the gainer. The only loser is the poor out-of-work specialist, whose occupation is gone.

WATSON [*laughs*].

HOLMES: Until a short while ago one's morning paper presented infinite possibilities. Often it was only the smallest trace, the faintest indication. To the scientific student of the higher criminal world no capital in Europe offered London's advantages. But now . . . You see! The newspaper lies unopened on my knee. Nothing tempts me to open it . . .

> [*The door bursts open and* MCFARLANE *rushes in*]

MCFARLANE: Mr. Sherlock Holmes?

WATSON: Who the devil . . . ?

MCFARLANE [*slightly off*]: Mr. Sherlock Holmes! [*Approaches quickly*] Please see me. Mr. Holmes, *I* am the unhappy John Hector McFarlane.

HOLMES: Indeed? Pray shut the door, Watson.

WATSON: Very well.

HOLMES: My friend the doctor here would no doubt prescribe a sedative for your symptoms.

> [*He pours a stiff drink from a decanter*]

So here it is.

MCFARLANE: Thank you [*he drinks*].

HOLMES: Now, Mr. McFarlane – you mentioned your name as if I should recognize it; but I assure you that beyond the obvious facts that you are a bachelor, a solicitor, a Freemason and an asthmatic I know nothing about you.

MCFARLANE: But . . . if you know all those things . . . !

HOLMES: Purely from observation. The . . . may I say . . . untidiness of the bachelor apparel; the sheaf of legal documents protruding from the jacket pocket; the Masonic watch-charm; and the asthmatical breathing. Quite straightforward, eh, Watson?

WATSON: Oh, quite, quite!

MCFARLANE: Well, I'm all that – and in addition I'm the most unfortunate man in London. I appeal to you, Mr. Holmes! If they come to arrest me before I've finished telling you my story please make them give me time to tell you the whole truth!

HOLMES: Arrest you? On what charge?

MCFARLANE: The murder of Mr. Jonas Oldacre.

WATSON: Murder!

HOLMES: Mr. McFarlane, it was only a moment ago that I was remarking to my friend that sensational cases had quite disappeared out of our newspapers.

MCFARLANE: Is that so! Then you haven't looked very closely at that one you have there! See! On the very front page!

HOLMES: Indeed! Watson, if you would be so good?

WATSON: Certainly, Holmes. [*Reads*] 'Mysterious affair at Lower Norwood. Suspicion of Murder and Arson. At about twelve o'clock last night an alarm was given that a stack of timber was on fire at the yard of Mr. Jonas Oldacre, a well-known builder. It was impossible to arrest the conflagration until the stack had been entirely consumed. Surprise was expressed at the absence of the owner of the establishment, and investigations revealed that a murderous struggle had apparently taken place in his room. An oaken walking-stick bore bloodstains on its handle, and a safe had been opened and papers scattered. It is known that Mr. Oldacre received a visitor yesterday evening, a young London solicitor named John Hector McFarlane, who is now being sought by the police for his help in their enquiries.'

MCFARLANE: You see? Now read out the Stop Press – there, below.

WATSON: Ah, yes. [*Reads*] 'There have been further and sinister developments in the investigation at Norwood, now in the experienced hands of Inspector Lestrade of Scotland Yard. Marks indicate that some bulky object had been dragged from the house to the burning wood-pile, in the ashes of which charred remains have been traced. The police theory is that the victim was clubbed to death in his room, his papers rifled, and his dead body dragged across to the wood-pile, which was then ignited so as to hide all traces of the crime.' Great heavens!

HOLMES: The case has certainly some points of interest. May I ask, Mr. McFarlane, how it is that you're still at liberty at all?

MCFARLANE: I live with my mother at Blackheath, but last night, having had to do business with Mr. Oldacre late in the evening, I stayed in an hotel at Norwood. I knew nothing of this horrible affair until I read that newspaper account in the train to the City. I hurried at once to put the case in your hands. As a matter of fact, I swear a man followed me out of London Bridge Station. I ...

[Knock at door]

WATSON: Come in!

[INSPECTOR LESTRADE *enters*]

Inspector Lestrade!

MCFARLANE: No! No!

LESTRADE: Dr. Watson. By your leave, Mr. Holmes . . . John Hector McFarlane, I arrest you for the wilful murder of Mr. Jonas Oldacre.

MCFARLANE: No!

LESTRADE: Anything you say will be taken down and may be put in evidence.

HOLMES: Lestrade – this gentleman was on the point of giving us an account of the affair, which might aid us in clearing it up.

LESTRADE: We'll have no difficulty doing that, Mr. Holmes.

HOLMES: Half an hour more or less can make no difference to you.

LESTRADE: Well, we owe you a good turn or two, Mr. Holmes. You've been of help to Scotland Yard once or twice ...

HOLMES: *Thank* you, Lestrade!

LESTRADE: Get on with your story, then, McFarlane.

MCFARLANE: Thank you, Inspector. I must explain first that I knew nothing of Jonas Oldacre, except that my parents had been acquainted with him many years ago. So I was very much surprised to get a request to go out to his home yesterday evening and advise him on a legal matter. I got to his house soon after nine and his house-keeper showed me into his room.

SCENE TWO

[*A 'flashback' as* MCFARLANE *enters* OLD-ACRE's *parlour*]

OLDACRE: Ah, my dear young sir! Do come in!

MCFARLANE: Thank you, sir.

OLDACRE: Very good of you to come all this way, Mr. McFarlane. I knew your parents many years ago, d'you know?

MCFARLANE: I have heard your name, sir, I'm sure.

OLDACRE: No doubt, no doubt. Well, now, to come straight to the point – I asked you here this evening to attend to my will.

MCFARLANE [*surprised*]: I see! But . . . then have you no solicitor of your own, sir?

OLDACRE: That is neither here nor there. If you will read the will for yourself, you will discover why I sent for you.

MCFARLANE: Very well.

OLDACRE [*amused*]: It's short and to the point, d'you see?

MCFARLANE: I . . . But . . . Mr. Oldacre! This will leaves your entire estate to . . . to *me*!

OLDACRE: Precisely. I am a bachelor, with hardly a living relation in the world. I knew your parents in my youth. As to yourself, I have always heard it said that you are diligent and thoroughly deserving. Therefore, I choose to make you my heir.

MCFARLANE: I don't know what to say.

OLDACRE: A simple word of thanks will do.

MCFARLANE: Oh! Of course! In my surprise, I . . . Mr. Oldacre, I do express my deepest gratitude to you.

OLDACRE: Quite enough! Now, simply assure me, as a lawyer, that the will is in proper form. I shall sign it, my housekeeper shall witness – and then we'll have supper.

MCFARLANE: With the greatest of pleasure, sir.

OLDACRE: After supper there are a number of papers – title-deeds, mortgages, scrip and so on – which I should like you to examine. You will inherit them all some day, and a few words of clarification now will save you endless searching when that time comes.

MCFARLANE: May that time be long delayed, sir!

OLDACRE: I share your wish, Mr. McFarlane. But, who can tell! And now, let us summon my housekeeper and proceed to the signing.

SCENE THREE

[The same scene some hours later]

MCFARLANE: You're tired, sir. I must be getting along.

OLDACRE: Well, I think everything is taken into account. I'll put all these papers back in the safe when you've gone. Goodness me, it's nearly twelve!

MCFARLANE: It's been a pleasure, sir.

OLDACRE: Indeed. Oh . . . ! Have you mislaid something?

MCFARLANE: My stick. Yes, I'm sure I had it with me.

OLDACRE: You did? I don't recall. Ah, well, my boy, I shall see a good deal of you now, I hope. If your stick turns up I'll keep it here until you can come back to claim it.

MCFARLANE: It'll be a great pleasure, sir. Once again, Mr. Oldacre – my warmest thanks, and, well, goodnight to you, sir.

SCENE FOUR

[*Back at 221B Baker Street*]

MCFARLANE: I left him there, the safe open, the papers in packets on the table. As I told you, I spent the night at the hotel in Norwood and knew nothing more until I read of this horrible affair in the morning paper.

LESTRADE: All right, then. Now, Mr. Holmes, anything you'd like to ask?

HOLMES: Not until I've been to Blackheath.

LESTRADE: Blackheath? You mean Norwood, don't you?

HOLMES [*amused*]: Oh, yes. No doubt that is what I must have meant.

LESTRADE [*calls*]: Constable!

CONSTABLE [*approaching*]: Sir?

LESTRADE: Take him away. I'll follow later.

MCFARLANE: Mr. . . . Mr. Holmes?

HOLMES: I shall do everything I can, Mr. McFarlane.

MCFARLANE: Thank you, sir. I put my trust in you.

CONSTABLE: Come on, this way.

[*He marches* MCFARLANE *away*]

LESTRADE: So, Mr. Holmes?

HOLMES: The case is not clear to me, Lestrade. What about you, Watson?

WATSON: Well . . . looks pretty clear-cut to me, I'm afraid.

LESTRADE: Exactly. Here's a young man who learns suddenly that if an older man dies he'll succeed to a fortune. He's alone with the old man, so there's the best chance he'll ever get. He murders him, burns his body

B

in the wood-pile, and then goes to an hotel nearby for the night. If that isn't clear, what *is*?

WATSON: Just what I'm thinking.

HOLMES: Yet it strikes me as being just a trifle *too* obvious. You don't add imagination to your other great qualities, my good Lestrade; but if you could for one moment put yourself in this young man's place, would you choose the very night the will had been signed to commit your crime?

LESTRADE: Well...

HOLMES: Would you choose an occasion when you're known by a servant to be in the house?

LESTRADE: Mm!

HOLMES: And would you, really, take the greatest pains to conceal the body, and yet leave your own stick lying about as a sign that you were the criminal?

WATSON: He was very likely afraid to go back to the room to look for it.

LESTRADE: All right, Mr. Holmes. Give me another theory that'd fit the facts.

HOLMES [*thoughtfully*]: I don't deny that the evidence favours your theory quite strongly, Lestrade. I only wish to point out that there *are* other theories possible.

LESTRADE: Well, I must be going. [*Going*] Look in at Norwood, if you're passing, and see how we're getting on.

[*He exits*]

WATSON: Mm! I must say, Holmes, he's got a strong case against that young fellow.

HOLMES [*going*]: The future will decide, Watson.

WATSON: What are we going to do?

HOLMES [*slightly off*]: As I said before, our first move must be in the direction of Blackheath.

WATSON: *Not* Norwood, then?

HOLMES [*approaching*]: Ah, Watson. We have in this case one singular incident coming close to the heels of another singular incident. The police are making the mistake of concentrating on the second of these, because it happens to be the one which is actually criminal. But it's evident to me that the *logical* way to approach the case is to try to throw some light on the first incident.

WATSON: You mean, the making of that curious will?

HOLMES: So suddenly, and to so unexpected an heir. Precisely. I think it may do something to simplify what followed.

WATSON: Yes, but what are we going to do at Blackheath?

HOLMES: Pay a visit upon our unfortunate young client's mother. Come, Watson. Get your coat like a good fellow.

SCENE FIVE

[MRS. MCFARLANE's *parlour*]

MRS. MCFARLANE [*sobbing*]: Of course my son is not guilty, Mr. Holmes! I won't admit even the possibility of it! As to Jonas Oldacre's fate, it neither surprises nor distresses me.

WATSON: Please calm yourself, Mrs. McFarlane...

MRS. MCFARLANE: He was more like a malignant and cunning ape than a human being: always – even as a young man.

HOLMES: Madam, please realize that to be heard speaking in such terms would only convince the police more deeply of your son's guilt.

MRS. MCFARLANE: I can't help it, Mr. Holmes! I hated that man. I regard his death as a blessing.

WATSON: You knew him from his youth?

MRS. MCFARLANE: I knew him *well*. He was after me to marry him. Thank Heaven I had the sense to refuse.

HOLMES: For any particular reason?

MRS. MCFARLANE: His cruelty. I had sensed something of it for myself: and then, one day, I heard how he had turned a cat loose in an aviary, simply to gloat over the destruction it would cause.

WATSON: Appalling!

MRS. MCFARLANE: I returned his ring at once.

HOLMES: What was his answer to that?

MRS. MCFARLANE [*turning slightly off*]: It was this.

[*Drawer opened*]

[*Turning back*] What do you think of that, gentlemen?

WATSON: It's your photograph – torn and . . . mutilated with some sharp instrument.

MRS. MCFARLANE: He sent it to me, with his curse, on the morning of my wedding to Mr. McFarlane.

WATSON: The villain!

HOLMES: I see! Had your son any knowledge of this?

MRS. MCFARLANE: No. Why?

HOLMES: Because the police would mark it down as providing an additional motive for him to have murdered this man – revenge for his past cruelty to you.

WATSON: And yet, Oldacre has left all his property to your son.

MRS. MCFARLANE: Neither my son nor I want anything

from Jonas Oldacre, dead or alive! I repeat, gentlemen, my son did not kill Jonas Oldacre.

SCENE SIX

[*221B Baker Street next day*]

HOLMES: It's all wrong, Watson. I *know* it's all wrong!

WATSON: But what do you deduce?

HOLMES: I examined Oldacre's bank-book amongst the other papers. His balance struck me as rather small for a man of such means, so I looked back through the entries during the last year. I found that a number of large cheques had been made out to a Mr. Cornelius. Yet this name does not appear in connection with any of the stocks and shares, or other papers.

WATSON: Won't Oldacre's bank help?

HOLMES: I very much hope so. It is the only line of enquiry left open to us. But I fear, my dear fellow, that our case will end ingloriously just the same with Lestrade hanging our client.

[*Knock at door, door opens*]

WATSON [*low*]: Speak of the devil!

LESTRADE: Mr. Holmes!

WATSON [*cheerfully*]: Come in, Inspector.

LESTRADE: Well, Mr. Holmes! Have you found your theory?

HOLMES [*stiffly*]: I have formed no conclusion whatever, Lestrade.

LESTRADE: Ah, but we formed ours yesterday, and now we're proved correct. [*Laughs*] You don't like being beaten, any more than the rest of us do – does he, Dr. Watson?

WATSON [*dignified*]: You certainly have the air of something unusual having occurred, Inspector.

LESTRADE: I've a cab outside. If you care to come with me to Norwood, gentlemen, I think I can convince you, once for all.

HOLMES [*sighs*]: Very well, Lestrade. I only hope you may be wrong.

SCENE SEVEN

[*In the hall of* OLDACRE'S *house*]

LESTRADE [*approaching*]: Now then. This is the late Old-acre's hall, and this is the hat rack where young McFarlane must have come to get his hat, after the crime was done.

HOLMES: Most likely.

LESTRADE: Now, look at this!

WATSON: A fingerprint – in blood!

LESTRADE: Actually a thumbprint, Doctor. Look at it through your lens, Mr. Holmes.

HOLMES: Yes, yes. I am doing.

LESTRADE: I'll just hold this next to it – the wax impression of McFarlane's thumb, taken this morning at my office.

HOLMES: Hm!

WATSON: It's ... the same?

HOLMES [*mock gloom*]: Dear me, dear me, Lestrade! It is a lesson in how deceptive appearances may be. And such a nice young man, it seemed.

LESTRADE [*triumphant*]: *Some* of us *are* a little too much inclined to be cocksure – *aren't* we, Mr. Holmes.

WATSON: Really!

HOLMES [*slyly*]: But what a providential thing that this young man should press his right thumb against the wall in taking his hat from the peg! Such a very *natural* action, too! By the way, Lestrade – who made this remarkable discovery?

LESTRADE: The housekeeper.

HOLMES: But why didn't the police see this mark earlier?

LESTRADE: Well, we'd no particular reason to examine the hall carefully.

HOLMES: I suppose there is no doubt that it *was* there earlier?

LESTRADE: Eh? Now, you're not going to suggest that McFarlane slipped specially out of gaol in order to make a print that would strengthen the evidence against himself! [*Going, laughing*] I'll be about the place, if you want me.

WATSON: Oh dear! It's all up for young McFarlane, then, Holmes.

HOLMES: On the contrary, Watson.

WATSON: Eh?

HOLMES: You see, there is one really serious flaw in this new discovery.

WATSON: What is it?

HOLMES: I examined this hall thoroughly myself, and I *know* that thumbprint was not there.

WATSON: What!

HOLMES: Now, come along. I wish to inspect this whole house, inside and out, and then we will trouble Lestrade to grant us one final indulgence.

SCENE EIGHT

[*The same scene, later*]

LESTRADE: Anything you like, Mr. Holmes! You'll acknow-
ledge we've been a little out in front of you this time, so
anything that'll help you understand our methods we'll
willingly arrange.

HOLMES: *Thank* you, Lestrade! As it happens, though, I
can't help thinking that your evidence is incomplete.

LESTRADE: Oh no! You're not going to start all over the
ground again!

HOLMES: By no means. Only, there *is* an important witness
you have not yet seen.

LESTRADE: Who? Can you produce him?

HOLMES: I think I can. How many constables have you?

LESTRADE: Two within call.

HOLMES: Both large, able-bodied men with powerful
voices?

WATSON: What have their voices to do with it, Holmes?

HOLMES: Perhaps I can help you to see that, and one or two
other things as well. Kindly summon them here, Lestrade, together with a considerable quantity of straw . . .

LESTRADE: *Straw?*

HOLMES: There's plenty in the outhouses. Oh, and a couple
of buckets of water.

LESTRADE: Now, look here, Mr. Holmes – if you know something, you can surely say it without all this tomfoolery!

HOLMES: I assure you, my good Lestrade, that I have an
excellent reason for everything I do. You may remember

chaffing me a little when the sun seemed to be on your side of the hedge? Well, you must not grudge me a little pomp and ceremony now. Be so kind as to carry out my request, and ask the constables to bring the things to the top landing of the house, as soon as possible.

SCENE NINE

[*On the top landing of* OLDACRE'S *house the policemen are setting down buckets of water and armfuls of straw*]

HOLMES: Just pile the straw together here, my good men.

FIRST CONSTABLE: Right y'are, sir.

HOLMES: Now, we have the buckets in readiness?

SECOND CONSTABLE: Over here, sir.

HOLMES: Capital! Will one of you open that window, please?

SECOND CONSTABLE: Yessir!

HOLMES: Watson...

WATSON: Yes, Holmes?

HOLMES: Have you a box of matches about you?

WATSON: Oh yes, of course! Somewhere here. Here you are.

HOLMES: Then kindly put a match to the edge of that straw.

WATSON: Holmes, I...

HOLMES: Watson!

WATSON: Oh, very well, Holmes.

[WATSON *does so*]

HOLMES: Now, as the draught from the window carries the smoke down the corridor, might I ask you all to join in the cry of 'Fire!'? Now – one, two, three...

ALL: Fire!

HOLMES: I'll trouble you once again. One, two, three . . .

ALL: Fire!!

HOLMES: Just once more, gentlemen, and all together. One, two, three . . .

ALL: FIRE!

> [*A concealed door in a wall flies open and* OLD-ACRE *runs out*]

OLDACRE: Help! Save me! For the love of Heaven, save me!

HOLMES: There he goes. Hold him, someone!

> [*The Policemen struggle with* OLDACRE *and overcome him*]

Watson, a bucket of water over that hay, if you please.

WATSON: Right, Holmes!

> [*He dashes a bucket of water over the burning straw, which is extinguished with a hiss*]

HOLMES: Thank you. Lestrade, allow me to present you with your missing witness – Mr. Jonas Oldacre.

LESTRADE: Eh! What! Oldacre?

OLDACRE: I've done no harm. You've got nothing against me.

HOLMES: No harm? You have done your best to get an innocent man hanged!

OLDACRE: It . . . it was only my practical joke.

LESTRADE: Oh, a joke was it? You won't find the laugh on your side, I promise you. Constable!

FIRST CONSTABLE: Sir?

LESTRADE: Take him down to the sitting-room and keep him there until I come. And watch him closely, all of you.

CONSTABLES: Yessir! [*Going*] Come on, and don't try nothing!

LESTRADE [*clearing throat*]: Mr. Holmes . . .

HOLMES: Yes, Lestrade?

LESTRADE: Mr. Holmes, I . . . I couldn't say anything before my constables, you understand, but I don't mind admitting this is the brightest thing you've ever done. You've saved an innocent man's life, and you've prevented a scandal that might've ruined my reputation in the Force.

HOLMES: Cheer up, Lestrade! Instead of being ruined, you'll find your reputation enhanced enormously. Just make a few alterations in your report, and they'll understand how hard it is to throw dust in the eyes of Inspector Lestrade.

LESTRADE [*hopefully*]: You . . . you don't want your name to appear?

HOLMES: Not at all. The work is its own reward. Perhaps I shall get the credit also at some distant day when my zealous historian here lays out the facts – eh, Watson?

WATSON: Too true, Holmes!

HOLMES: Well, now, let's see where that rat has been lurking.

LESTRADE: Yes! That door he suddenly came out of – I'd never noticed it.

HOLMES [*slightly off*]: Because it was so well concealed. He's a builder, remember? [*Approaching*] See here – this little lath and plaster compartment.

WATSON [*slightly off*]: Jove! A chair, a lamp; food and books . . . !

HOLMES: He was able to fix up his own little hiding-place without any confederate – save that precious housekeeper of his, of course. I should lose no time in adding her to your bag, by the way, Lestrade.

LESTRADE: Don't worry. She won't get far.

WATSON [*approaching*]: But Holmes – how on earth did you know he was in the house at all?

HOLMES: The thumb-mark. I knew it had not been there earlier. Therefore, it had been made since.

WATSON: But how? I mean, McFarlane was under lock and key!

HOLMES: Very simply. When they were sealing those documents up after going through them together, Oldacre got McFarlane to secure one of the seals by pressing his thumb into the hot wax. Perhaps it wasn't even contrived deliberately at all. But later, it suddenly struck him what absolutely damning evidence he could make against McFarlane by using it. It was the simplest thing in the world to get his housekeeper to fetch him the seal and some wax, from which he made an impression. Then all he had to do was moisten it with as much blood as he could get from a pin-prick in his own finger and get her to impress the mark on the wall when nobody was about.

LESTRADE: It's wonderful!

WATSON: It's remarkable!

LESTRADE: Clear as crystal when you put it like that! But what's it all about, all this business?

HOLMES: You know that Oldacre was once refused by McFarlane's mother...

LESTRADE: I didn't know that!

HOLMES: Dear me! I *told* you to go to Blackheath first and Norwood afterwards. All his life he's longed for vengeance, and now he suddenly finds himself in a bad way financially – rash speculation, I imagine. To save himself, Oldacre pays large cheques to a Mr. Cornelius, who I've no doubt is himself. He intends to disappear under that name, thus escaping his creditors once and for all.

WATSON: And contrived his 'death' to put them off his scent!

HOLMES: Not only that – he could take an ample and crushing revenge on his former sweetheart by making it appear that his murder had been committed by her only child.

WATSON: Monstrous!

HOLMES: He cast a net round young McFarlane from which, until a short while ago, it seemed impossible that there could be any escape.

LESTRADE: But he didn't know when to stop.

HOLMES: That supreme gift of the artist was lacking. He wished to improve what was already perfect: to draw the rope tighter yet round his victim's neck. And, in so doing, he ruined all.

LESTRADE: Diabolical! Mr. Holmes, I congratulate you!

WATSON: And so do I Holmes. But, er . . .

HOLMES: Oh, dear! What have I omitted now, Watson?

WATSON: Well, I can understand how he managed to hide McFarlane's stick that night, so it would be found later; and how he contrived to get a few bloodstains about the place . . .

HOLMES: What then?

WATSON: But what about the charred remains they found? I mean to say . . .

HOLMES: I'll tell you what, my dear Watson – if ever you should write an account of this case, and find it necessary to account both for the blood *and* for the charred remains I suggest you make a brace of rabbits and some trouser buttons serve your turn.

THE DISAPPEARANCE OF LADY FRANCES CARFAX

Characters in order of appearance:

SHERLOCK HOLMES

DR. WATSON

M. MOSER: French-Swiss manager of a Lausanne hotel.

HERR DIETRICH: German manager of an hotel at Baden Baden.

RECEPTIONIST (French) at an hotel in Montpelier.

MARIE DEVINE: Lady Frances Carfax's former French maid.

THE HON. PHILIP GREEN: a tough, rather wild man of middle age.

'HOLY PETERS': an Australian confidence trickster.

ANNIE: his 'wife'.

POLICE SERGEANT

UNDERTAKER

THE DISAPPEARANCE OF
LADY FRANCES CARFAX

SCENE ONE

> [HOLMES *and* WATSON *are seated at their ease in the parlour of 221B Baker Street*]

HOLMES: But why Turkish, my dear Watson? Why Turkish?

WATSON: Turkish? My boots, Holmes?

HOLMES: No, no, no – I mean the bath. Why the relaxing and expensive Turkish, rather than the invigorating home-made article?

WATSON: Oh, for the simple reason that for the past few days I've been feeling rheumaticky and old.

HOLMES: Really, Watson?

WATSON: By the way, Holmes, I've no doubt the connection between my boots and a Turkish bath is clear enough to a logical mind like yours, but I would be obliged if you'd let me in on the secret.

HOLMES: You are in the habit of doing up your boots in a certain way. I see them on this occasion fastened with an elaborate double bow. Who has tied them for you? A bootmaker? Unlikely. The boots are not new. So what remains? Only, I fancy, the attendant at the bath.

WATSON [*chuckles*]: Remarkable!

HOLMES: Well, for all that, the Turkish bath has served quite another purpose.

WATSON: Oh? What's that?

HOLMES: It led you to tell me you needed a change. Let

C

me suggest that you take one. How would Lausanne do?

WATSON: Lausanne!

HOLMES: First-class tickets and all expenses paid – on a princely scale.

WATSON: Splendid! But, what's it all about, Holmes?

HOLMES: One of the most dangerous classes in this world, my dear Watson, is the drifting and friendless woman; she is the inevitable inciter of crime in others.

WATSON: How so?

HOLMES: She has sufficient means to take her from country to country and from hotel to hotel. She is lost, as often as not, in a maze of obscure *pensions* and boarding-houses – a stray chicken in a world of foxes, Watson, and when she is gobbled up she's hardly missed. Hm! I very much fear some evil has come to the Lady Frances Carfax.

WATSON: Aha, so now we descend from the general to the particular.

HOLMES: Lady Frances is the sole survivor of the direct family of the late Earl of Rufton. She was left with limited means, but with some very remarkable old Spanish jewellery. She refused to leave them in the bank and always carried them about with her.

WATSON: What sort of a woman is she, then?

HOLMES: Rather pathetic. Beautiful, still in fresh middle age. But all the same she is the last derelict of what only twenty years ago was a goodly fleet.

WATSON: So what has happened to her?

HOLMES: All I can tell you is that for four years it has been her custom to write every second week to her old governess, Miss Dobney, who lives in Camberwell. It is Miss Dobney who has consulted me. Nearly five weeks have passed without a word. The last letter was from the *Hotel Nationale* at Lausanne. Lady Frances seems to have left there and given no address.

WATSON: Surely she had other correspondents.

HOLMES: There is one correspondent who is a sure draw, Watson – her bank. Single ladies' pass-books are compressed diaries. I have been able to glance over her account. The last cheque drawn was to a Miss Marie Devine. It was cashed at the *Credit Lyonnais* less than three weeks ago. The sum was fifty pounds.

WATSON: D'you know who Miss Marie Devine is?

HOLMES: Yes. Lady Frances Carfax's maid. Why she should have paid her this cheque we have not yet determined. No doubt your researches will soon clear that up.

WATSON: *My* researches?

HOLMES: Hence the health-giving expedition to Lausanne. One or two matters prevent me from leaving the country just at the moment. Besides, on general principles it's best for me not to go. Scotland Yard feels lonely without me, and it causes an unhealthy excitement among the criminal classes.

WATSON: Really, Holmes! [*Chuckles*]

HOLMES: You'll go, then?

WATSON: Of course.

HOLMES: Good luck, then. And if my humble counsel can ever be valued at so extravagant a rate as twopence a word it waits your disposal night and day at the end of the Continental wire.

SCENE TWO

[*The foyer of an hotel in Lausanne.* WATSON *is questioning the manager,* M. MOSER]

MOSER: Oh, yes, but certainly, Monsieur Watson, me Lady Carfax was very much liked by all my staff. A charming lady, monsieur. She was very happy 'ere in Lausanne.

WATSON: Yet she left quite suddenly, I understand, Monsieur Moser.

MOSER: That I cannot comprehend. She 'as no intention to leave. Then suddenly comes this *sauvage*.

WATSON: *Sauvage?* Oh, savage. Who was he?

MOSER: That I cannot say. He come to visit me lady a day or two before she go away. Big, and black of the beard. But me lady will not see 'im. Then, next day, *pouf*! She goes.

WATSON: What nationality?

MOSER: Oh, *Anglais*.

WATSON: You mean English. Well, you've been very helpful indeed, Monsieur Moser. There is just one more thing, though. When Lady Frances left, did her maid accompany her?

MOSER: Marie Devine? No, she 'as gone to Montpelier.

WATSON: To another situation?

MOSER: Yes, monsieur. Here is 'er address.

WATSON: Thank you. Very well, then, I must go there, too. Thank you again, monsieur. Er, *merci. Merci beaucoup.*

MOSER: The pleasure is mine, sir.

SCENE THREE

[WATSON *is reading out telegram as he writes it*]

WATSON: Sherlock Holmes. 221B Baker Street, London. Before proceeding shall visit Baden Baden. Have ascertained Lady Frances despatched luggage there by roundabout route before leaving Lausanne. Regards, Watson.

SCENE FOUR

[*At the Englischer Hof Hotel, Baden Baden,* WATSON *is interviewing the manager,* HERR DIETRICH]

DIETRICH: Oh, ja, ja, Herr Doktor – de Lady Carfax was here for ten days. She is gone away three weeks since.

WATSON: I see. Have you any idea what she did with her time here in Baden Baden, Herr Dietrich? I mean, did she strike up acquaintance with any other guests here?

DIETRICH: Oh, yes, there was Doktor Shlessinger and his wife. They have a very good friendship made with the Lady Carfax.

WATSON: Dr. Shlessinger? A German doctor?

DIETRICH: Nein, he was from Souss America, he and his wife were – er, what you call it? – missionaires.

WATSON: Oh no. Missionaries.

DIETRICH: Ah, thank you. The Lady Carfax, you know, is

very much religious, so they are become friends very quick. The Doktor Shlessinger has been sick, you know, and he sits all the days here in his chair on this terrace and makes the map of the Holy Land.

WATSON: Good heavens!

DIETRICH: With him every day is his wife and the Lady Carfax. These two ladies, they nurse him, and he is got better again. He and his wife go back to London, and the other lady too.

WATSON: They all went to London?

DIETRICH: Ja, all go. Doktor Shlessinger pays the bill for them all.

WATSON: One more question, Herr Dietrich – has any other person inquired here for Lady Carfax since she left?

DIETRICH: Er – oh, ja! A week ago, an Englishman. Very ... very ...

WATSON: *Sauvage*?

DIETRICH: Savage! Exact! With the beard and of the face very fierce. Oh, ja, savage, very savage.

SCENE FIVE

[WATSON *is at an hotel reception desk in Montpelier*]

RECEPTIONIST: I 'ope your stay in Montpelier will be most pleasant, Monsieur Watson. Oh, 'ere is a telegram for you, from London.

WATSON [*reads*]: 'Progress capital. A credit to my training. Please wire description of Shlessinger's left ear. Holmes.' Eh? Shlessinger's left ear.

SCENE SIX

[MARIE DEVINE'S *home. She and* WATSON
are in a room facing the street]

MARIE DEVINE: I tell you quite true, Docteur Watson, I
'ave only left my lady because I will marry soon. When
I see 'er at last in good 'ands with le Docteur Shlessinger
and Madame, well I think the good time is now come.

WATSON: But you were friends with Lady Frances when you
left her, Miss Devine?

DEVINE: Of course! She give me fifty pounds for the wedding
present.

WATSON: Yes, well, to go back to this savage-looking man
with the beard . . . do you think it possible your mistress
left Lausanne to get away from him?

DEVINE: Yes, yes! It is true, I know. Me lady is nothing said
to me, but I can see, she is afraid. [*Pause*] *Mon Dieu*!

WATSON: What's the matter? Miss Devine!

DEVINE: *Sacré nom*! Out of the window. See!

WATSON: Eh? Where?

DEVINE: There – it is he, with the beard.

WATSON: Good Lord!

DEVINE: Oh, monsieur, what is he doing here?

WATSON: Well at the moment he appears to be looking at
the house numbers. You're sure he's the one?

DEVINE: Oh, yes, yes.

WATSON: Then I suppose he was proposing to pay you a
visit. Why would that be?

DEVINE: I don't know, monsieur. Oh, monsieur, I am afraid.

WATSON: Don't worry. I'll go out and have a word with him myself. You stay here.

> [WATSON *hurries into the busy street to accost the stranger*]

Excuse me! May I ask if you are an Englishman?

GREEN: Yes, I am. What about it?

WATSON: May I ask your name?

GREEN: You certainly may not!

WATSON: I see. Perhaps, then, you will tell me where I can find the Lady Frances Carfax?

GREEN [*roars*]: Why, you . . . !

> [*They struggle. Spectators gather round but a street-cleaner pushes his way through and rescues* WATSON, *sending* GREEN *on his way*]

HOLMES: *Monsieur, monsieur – je viens vous aider! Va t'en! Va t'en!*

WATSON [*puffing*]: Uh! Ah! Er, *merci – merci beaucoup, monsieur.*

HOLMES: *Il n'y a pas de quoi, monsieur.* [*Own voice, low*] Watson, listen to me!

WATSON: Holmes!

HOLMES: Quietly, man. You've made a pretty enough hash of things already. [*Loudly*] *Ah, monsieur, il me faut vous accompagner à votre hotel.* Let's get away before some gendarme gets curious. Lead on to your hotel; quickly now.

WATSON [*crestfallen*]: Very well, Holmes. [*Loudly*] Ah, *merci, monsieur. Encore, merci beaucoup . . .*

SCENE SEVEN

[WATSON'S *room in his hotel a few minutes later*]

HOLMES: Well, Watson, a nice mess you've made of things.

WATSON: Now, look here, Holmes . . .

HOLMES: I cannot at the moment recall any possible blunder you've omitted. All you have done is to give the alarm everywhere and discover nothing.

WATSON: No doubt you would have done better.

HOLMES: I *have* done better.

WATSON: Eh?

HOLMES: You'll see in a moment. I'm expecting a visitor.

WATSON: In *my* room?

HOLMES: I sent word to him from the reception desk as we came up.

WATSON: Very well. But, look here, you might at least tell me how you came to be near that girl's house, dressed in that road-sweeper's get-up, just in time to butt in. Er, thanks, by the way.

HOLMES: My dear Watson, think nothing of it. I sensed that things weren't going too well – you have been a bit tactless, you know – and when I found I was able to get away from London after all I decided to head you off at the earliest opportunity. I was going to intercept you when you left the girl's house. I didn't bargain for anything quite so dramatic, though.

[*A knock at the door*]

Ah, I fancy this will be our visitor. He's a fellow-lodger of yours in this hotel.

[GREEN *enters*]

Ah, come in, my dear sir.

GREEN: Thank you.

WATSON [*to himself*]: Good lord! The savage!

HOLMES [*approaching*]: This is the Honourable Philip Green, Watson. Mr. Green, this is Doctor Watson, my old friend and associate. [*They greet one another*] He's helping us in this affair. But, of course, you've already met.

GREEN: I hope I didn't hurt you, Dr. Watson? Of course, if I'd known . . .

WATSON: I must say, sir, I don't understand . . .

GREEN: When you came up to me like that, and started asking questions about Frances, so – so accusingly, I admit I lost my grip. My nerves these days are like live wires. But all this business is beyond me.

WATSON: And me.

HOLMES: I had better tell you, then, Mr. Green, that I learned of your existence through Miss Dobney, Lady Frances' old governess.

GREEN: Old Susan Dobney, with the mob cap! I remember her well.

HOLMES: That would be in the days before you found it better to go to South Africa?

GREEN: What! [*Pause*] Yes, I see you know my story, then, Mr. Holmes. Very well. You see, there was never a young man in this world loved a woman more than I loved Frances. The trouble was – well, I'd always been a pretty wild youngster, and when she got to hear of some of my goings-on she had nothing more to do with me. And yet when I came back, all these years after, and heard she was unmarried still, I . . . well, I found her at Lausanne. I tried all I knew to convince her I was a changed man. She was weakening a bit, I think, but when I called again she'd left the town. When I heard her maid was here in Montpelier, I thought I'd find out what she knew. But now, Mr. Holmes, if you do know anything about Lady Frances, for Heaven's sake please tell me it!

HOLMES: You can rest assured that everything possible will be done. What is your London address?

GREEN: The Langham Hotel will find me.

HOLMES: Then may I recommend you return there and be on hand in case I want you? Watson, if you will pack your bag I will cable to Mrs. Hudson to make one of her best efforts for two hungry travellers arriving at 221B Baker Street at seven-thirty tomorrow.

SCENE EIGHT

[*221B Baker Street next day*]

WATSON: Holmes, here's a telegram for you. From Baden Baden.

[HOLMES *opens it*]

HOLMES: Ha! From your friend Herr Dietrich, manager of the Englischer Hof. Here you are.

WATSON [*reads*]: 'Jagged or torn'. That's all it says. 'Jagged or torn.' What on earth, Holmes . . .

HOLMES: A description of Shlessinger's left ear. I thought you might have left Baden by the time my inquiry reached you, so I sent a duplicate to Herr Dietrich.

WATSON: What does it show, then?

HOLMES: It shows, as I suspected, that the Reverend Dr. Shlessinger, missionary from South America, is none other than Holy Peters, one of the most unscrupulous rascals that ever came out of Australia.

WATSON: Good lord!

HOLMES: His particular speciality is the beguiling of lonely ladies by playing upon their religious feelings. His so-called wife, an Englishwoman called Fraser, helps him.

WATSON: How on earth did you guess that?

HOLMES: It was no guess. The nature of Shlessinger's tactics suggested his identity at once. I knew Holy Peters had been badly bitten about the ear in a saloon fight in Adelaide in '89, so this telegram confirms my suspicion. This poor Lady Frances is in the hands of an infernal couple, Watson. They'll stick at nothing.

WATSON: Not murder?

HOLMES: I'm afraid it's more than likely she is dead already. If not, she's undoubtedly in some sort of captivity.

WATSON: Perhaps she never even got here to London with Shlessinger and his . . . this other woman.

HOLMES: On the other hand, if she is alive, all my instincts tell me they'll have her here. I suggest we eat our dinner, then I will take the obvious step of strolling down to Scotland Yard and asking our friend Lestrade to keep a look out for us. Then we must possess our souls in patience, and hope we have some news for Mr. Green before very much longer.

> [*The door is flung open and* GREEN *enters agitatedly*]

WATSON: Mr. Green!

GREEN: Mr. Holmes, I've seen the woman – in the Westminster Road. I followed her into a pawnbroker's. She sold a pendant and some other jewels.

WATSON: Belonging to Lady Frances Carfax?

GREEN: Without a doubt!

HOLMES: You didn't intervene, though?

GREEN: No. She got a cab and I followed her in another.

HOLMES: Excellent!

GREEN: She got down at No. 36 Poultney Square, Brixton. I drove round the corner and walked back to the house. But just then a van came up and two men started to unload it. I saw what they took out, Mr. Holmes. It was a coffin.

WATSON: Great heavens!

GREEN: They carried it up to the door of No. 36 and the woman let them in with it. I thought for a moment of rushing in. But I remembered my promise to you and came straight back here.

HOLMES: You've done excellent work, Mr. Green.

GREEN: The coffin, Mr. Holmes. Do you think . . .

HOLMES: Not a moment will be lost. But we can do nothing legal without a warrant, and if you want to help further you'll take the note I shall write down to the authorities and get one.

GREEN: Gladly.

HOLMES: As for us, Watson, there is not a moment to be lost getting to Poultney Square. Mr. Green will set the regular forces on the move. We, as usual, are the irregulars, and we must take our own line of action. The situation is desperate and extreme measures are justified.

SCENE NINE

[*The street outside No. 36 Poultney Square*]

HOLMES: This is the house, Watson. No. 36.

[*He rings the doorbell*]

WATSON: What about the police? And the warrant?

HOLMES: There is no time to waste, keeping within the four corners of the law. We must just take our chance together, as so often in the past.

WATSON: I'm with you, Holmes.

[PETERS *answers the door*]

PETERS: Gentlemen?

HOLMES: You are Henry Peters, of Adelaide, late the Rev. Dr. Shlessinger, of Baden and South America. I am Sherlock Holmes. I want to know what you have done with the Lady Frances Carfax.

PETERS [*laughs*]: Oh, is that it? I'd be very glad if *you* could tell *me* where she is. She attached herself on to Mrs. Peters and me at Baden and she stuck on to us till London. I paid her bill and her ticket. Once in London she gave us the slip. You find her, Mr. Holmes, and I'm in your debt.

HOLMES: I *mean* to find her. I'm going through this house till I do find her.

ANNIE [*approaching*]: Henry? What's happened?

PETERS: Ah, Annie, there you are, my love. Go fetch a policeman, will you?

ANNIE: All right, love. Take care, though. I won't be a jiff.

WATSON: Holmes . . .

HOLMES: Let her go, Watson. It merely means our time is limited. Now, Peters, where is that coffin?

PETERS: What do you want with the coffin?

HOLMES: I want to see the body inside it.

PETERS: Not with my consent, you won't.

HOLMES: Without it, then.

PETERS: Oh, have it your own way. It's in here.

[*They enter the house*]

HOLMES: Thank you. Have the goodness to turn up the lights, Watson.

PETERS: Oh, do allow me!

HOLMES: Thank you. And now, let's take a look.

[*The coffin lid is unfastened and raised*]

WATSON: Lady Frances?

HOLMES: I think not.

WATSON: Thank Heaven!

PETERS: Blundered for once, haven't you?

HOLMES: Who is this, Peters?

PETERS: It's an old nurse of my wife's. Rose Spender, she was called. We found her in Brixton Workhouse Infirmary, and like Christian folk we brought her here to die. Mind you take the address of the doctor who's been to see her – it's Dr. Horsom, of 13 Firbank Villas.

WATSON: Horsom? Yes, I know him.

PETERS: She died after three days. He signed the certificate. Senile decay – only, of course, that's only a doctor's opinion. Sherlock Holmes'd know better, eh? Anyway, Stimson and Company of the Kennington Road are burying her at eight tomorrow morning. Pick any holes in that lot, Mr. Holmes?

HOLMES: Just the same, I'm going through your house.

[*Men's voices are heard approaching*]

SERGEANT: This way, ma'am?

ANNIE: Yes, in here officers.

PETERS: Are you through? [*Calling*] This way, officers, if you please. These men have forced their way into my house, and I can't get rid of them.

SERGEANT [*approaching*]: Now, then, what's it all about?

HOLMES: Here is my card, Sergeant.

SERGEANT: Well, of course, sir, we know all about you, sir. But you can't stay here without a warrant, sir.

HOLMES: I quite understand that.

PETERS: Arrest them!

SERGEANT: We know where to lay our hands on this gentleman if he's wanted, sir. But you'll have to go, Mr. Holmes.

HOLMES [*disappointed*]: Yes, Watson, we shall have to go. Come along, my dear fellow.

SCENE TEN

[*Next morning* WATSON'S *bedroom clock is chiming as* HOLMES *shakes him awake*]

HOLMES: Watson, Watson! Wake up quickly!

WATSON [*yawns*]: I am awake! Just going to get up.

HOLMES: What time was the funeral to be? Eight wasn't it?

WATSON: Funeral? Yes, eight, that's it. Holmes, what on earth's the matter?

HOLMES: I should have seen it sooner. The funeral is at eight, and it's now approaching seven-twenty. I'll never forgive myself if we're too late. Now come on, for Heaven's sake! It's life or death, I tell you!

SCENE ELEVEN

[HOLMES *and* WATSON *run up the street to No. 36 Poultney Square*]

WATSON: Thank heaven! The hearse! Still standing outside the house.

HOLMES: Yes, and there comes the coffin. [*Calling*] Right, my good men. Take that coffin back inside at once, if you please!

PETERS: Here, what the devil are you up to? Interfering again, are you, and in a Christian funeral this time!

HOLMES: A warrant is on its way, Peters. Come along, my men.

UNDERTAKER: Well, I dunno . . .

HOLMES: Do as I tell you, or you'll be sorry! This is police work.

UNDERTAKER: Eh! Oh, police work! Fred! You 'eard the gent. To you, now – and careful!

SCENE TWELVE

[*Inside the house*]

HOLMES: Put it down here. Now, there's a sovereign for you if the lid's off in one minute.

UNDERTAKER: Come on, Fred!

WATSON: Peters has slipped off somewhere, Holmes. Want me to take a look?

D

HOLMES: Never mind him, Watson. There may be work for you here.

[*The lid is jerked off*]

UNDERTAKER: There y'are, sir. Cor! What a stink!

WATSON: It's chloroform, Holmes!

UNDERTAKER: Lor luv us, there's two of 'em!

HOLMES: And the second, if I'm not mistaken, Watson, is the lady for whom we've been seeking. The point is, are we in time?

WATSON: Let me see? I can't tell. It's saturated with chloroform. Artificial respiration's the only chance. Holmes, send a fellow off in a cab to the nearest surgery, will you? I must have some ether, and a syringe. I'll get to work as best I can in the meanwhile.

SCENE THIRTEEN

[*Inside the house*]

HOLMES: Capital, my dear Watson! Splendid work.

WATSON [*puffed*]: Well, it was touch and go, Holmes. Another few minutes . . .

HOLMES: Ah, yes. But she's safe now?

WATSON: Completely. She'll be in a hospital bed by now, if they've got a move on. Jove, Holmes, that coffin was almost swimming in chloroform!

HOLMES: They meant to make sure.

WATSON: Well, perhaps now this poor little old workhouse lady can have her funeral after all.

HOLMES: At least she'll have her coffin to herself.

WATSON: Yes, she looks quite lost in it.

HOLMES: That, my dear Watson, is an observation I wish you had made when friend Peters first showed her to us the other day.

WATSON: Well, you saw her, too, Holmes.

HOLMES: Yes, and should you care to add this case to your annals, Watson, you may put it down as an example of temporary eclipse of the mind. I spent the whole of last night trying to hit on the clue which I knew would bring us the solution to this case. And all the time it was here – this over-large coffin for this tiny, wasted old woman.

WATSON: Specially ordered, you mean – to leave room for Lady Frances's body, too?

HOLMES: Exactly. They would both have been buried under the one certificate. Even if there ever had been an exhumation – which wasn't very likely – there would have been no marks of violence on her. In any case, Peters would have been through half a dozen other aliases by then.

WATSON: It's horrible, Holmes! They kept that poor lady captive all this time, and then, when they'd got all they needed from her, this was their way of disposing of her! Of all the cold-blooded fiends I ever heard of . . .

HOLMES: Fiendish, but very, very clever. Quite new in the annals of crime, I should say. It's too much to expect, I suppose, that they'll have escaped the hands of our Scotland Yard friends. Such brilliant originality could have kept us happily engaged for years to come, my dear Watson. Eh? Don't you agree . . . ?

WATSON: Oh, really, Holmes!

SHOSCOMBE OLD PLACE

Characters in order of appearance:

SHERLOCK HOLMES

DR. WATSON

JOHN MASON: Sir Robert Norberton's head trainer. A blunt, straight-spoken man in his early forties.

STEPHENS: Sir Robert Norberton's coachman. A few years younger than Mason; rather weedy and timid.

JOSIAH BARNES: Landlord of the Green Dragon Inn, Crendall. Elderly.

LODGEKEEPER

SIR ROBERT NORBERTON: A peppery landowner.

NORLETT: Sir Robert Norberton's footman.

SHOSCOMBE OLD PLACE

SCENE ONE

> [*The parlour of 221B Baker Street one morning late in May.* HOLMES *and* WATSON *are taking their ease after breakfast*]

HOLMES: You know something of racing, don't you, Watson?

WATSON: I ought to, Holmes. I pay for it with about half my wound pension.

HOLMES: Then I shall make you my 'Handy Guide to the Turf'. Does the name Sir Robert Norberton recall anything?

WATSON: Of Shoscombe Old Place? Once horsewhipped Sam Brewer, the Curzon Street moneylender, on Newmarket Heath?

HOLMES: That's the man.

WATSON: He nearly killed him. Mm! He's one of those fellows who should have been a Regency buck. Great eye for the ladies; boxer, athlete, rider. Came second in the National a few years ago.

HOLMES: Ah!

WATSON: But they say he's lost a fortune on the Turf as well.

HOLMES: So? Can you give me some idea of Shoscombe Old Place?

WATSON: In Berkshire. The Shoscombe stud and training quarters are there.

HOLMES: And the head trainer is John Mason. You needn't

look surprised, my dear Watson. He was due here some minutes ago. But do let us have some more about Shoscombe. I seem to have struck a rich vein.

WATSON: Well, there are the Shoscombe spaniels, Holmes. You hear of them at every dog show. They're the special pride of the Lady of Shoscombe Old Place.

HOLMES: Sir Robert Norberton's wife?

WATSON: Oh, no, no, he's never married. He lives with his widowed sister, Lady Beatrice Falder. The place belonged to her late husband. Norberton has no claim on it at all. When she dies it reverts to her husband's brother.

HOLMES: So she only has a life interest in it?

WATSON: That's right. She draws the rents and Norberton spends them. Still, I have heard that she's devoted to him.

HOLMES: Capital, Watson! An admirable thumb-nail sketch.

[*There is a knock at the door*]

And here, I expect, is the man who can fill in the detail. Come in!

[JOHN MASON *enters*]

MASON: Mr. Holmes?

HOLMES: Come in, Mr. Mason. This is my friend and colleague, Dr. Watson.

MASON: How d'ye do, sir?

WATSON: How d'ye do?

[*Door shut*]

MASON [*approaching*]: You had my note, Mr. Holmes?

HOLMES: Yes, but it explained nothing.

MASON: It was too delicate to put on paper. And too complicated.

HOLMES: Well, here we are, at your disposal. Take a seat, Mr. Mason.

MASON: Thank you. First of all, Mr. Holmes, I think my employer, Sir Robert Norberton, has gone mad.

HOLMES: This is Baker Street, not Harley Street. But why do you say that?

MASON: Well, sir, when a man does one or two odd things, there may be a meaning to it. But when everything he does is odd, you begin to wonder. I reckon Shoscombe Prince and the Derby between them have turned his brain.

WATSON: Shoscombe Prince is a colt Sir Robert has entered, Holmes.

MASON: The best in England. But I'll be plain with you gentlemen, because I know this won't go beyond the room.

WATSON: Quite right!

MASON: Sir Robert has got to win this Derby. It's his last chance. Everything he can raise or borrow is on that horse – and at big odds, too.

WATSON: Big odds? With a horse as good as that . . . ?

MASON: Ah! The public don't know how good he is, Dr. Watson. Sir Robert has the Prince's half-brother out for spins. You can't tell 'em apart.

WATSON: I see!

MASON: But there are two lengths in a furlong between 'em when it comes to a gallop. If the Prince fails him, he's done.

HOLMES: It seems a rather desperate gamble. But where does madness come in?

MASON: You've only got to look at him. His eyes are wild.

He's down at the stables at all hours. Then there's the way he behaves to Lady Beatrice.

WATSON: What is that?

MASON: They've always been the best of friends. She loves the horses as much as he does. Called to see Shoscombe Prince every day. But that's all over now.

HOLMES: Why?

MASON: For a week she's driven past the stables without so much as a 'Good morning' to me or anyone.

HOLMES: You suspect a quarrel?

MASON: Why else would he give away her own pet spaniel?

WATSON: *Her* spaniel?

MASON: She loved it as if it was her child. But he gave it away a few days ago to old Barnes, who keeps the Green Dragon near Crendall.

WATSON: Strange indeed.

MASON: Of course, what with her weak heart and dropsy she couldn't get about with Sir Robert, but he used to spend a couple of hours with her in her room every evening. But that's all over, too. He never goes anywhere near her. Everything's changed, Mr. Holmes, and something's going on, mark my words.

HOLMES: There is something more, then?

MASON: That there is, sir. Night after night the master sneaks off down to the crypt at the old ruined church in the park. There's not many in our parts would think of going there by night.

WATSON: Haunted, no doubt?

MASON: Ah, you may smile, Doctor. It's had a bad name amongst us for generations. Anyway, there he goes every night, wet or fine.

HOLMES: You get more and more interesting, Mr. Mason. But how do you know all this?

MASON: Well, it was Stephens, the coachman, noticed him sneaking off first of all and told me. None of our business, perhaps you'll say, but we went after him. We waited behind a bush and saw him go inside the crypt. He was gone a long time.

SCENE TWO

[*A 'flashback' to the night in question;* MASON *and* STEPHENS *hiding near the old crypt entrance*]

MASON [*speaking low*]: This is jumpy work, all right, Fred. It'll be a bad job for us if he spots us.

STEPHENS: He's no respecter of persons when he gets started. Still, I mean to see this out, Mr. Mason.

MASON: Well, we shan't see much from here.

STEPHENS: Hey! He's coming out now.

MASON: Keep down then. He'll come past these bushes. Ssh!

[SIR ROBERT NORBERTON *passes without seeing them*]

STEPHENS: Well, he wasn't carrying nothing. So where does that get us?

MASON: Fred, I'm going to take a look inside. Come on.

STEPHENS: In-inside! Oh. I dunno, Mr. Mason.

MASON: Come on, man. If master can go in there and come out safe, I reckon we can.

STEPHENS: Well...

MASON: Wait out here for me, if you like.

STEPHENS: No, I'll come. [*Hopefully*] Door'll be locked, anyway.

[MASON *tries the handle. The door squeaks open*]

MASON: Well, it isn't.

STEPHENS [*disappointed*]: Oh!

[*They enter the stony crypt*]

MASON [*whispers*]: Can't hear anything. Don't reckon there's anyone else here.

STEPHENS: Down the steps, then. There's nothing up here.

MASON: Righto. Got your lantern?

STEPHENS: Hang on while I light up. That's it.

[*They step cautiously down the stone steps*]

Well, there's no one there.

MASON: No one and nothing.

STEPHENS: Then that's that. We can be getting back.

MASON: What's that over there?

STEPHENS [*startled*]: What?

MASON: Now that's funny.

STEPHENS: It's – it's bones. Bones and a-a-a skull!

MASON: It is, too. Now, I was down here some time back when the master sent Higgins to see those gypsies weren't camping out in the place. And these weren't there then.

STEPHENS: Mr. Mason . . . you don't reckon . . .

MASON: No, they're old bones, these. Might be hundreds of years old. But where've they come from? Why should anyone drag 'em out and leave them lying like this? This beats me, Fred. It beats me.

SCENE THREE

[*221B as before*]

MASON: And beat us both, it did, Mr. Holmes.

HOLMES: You left the bones where they were?

MASON: Yes. Lying in a corner, with a bit of old board over them. But now, take a look at this.

HOLMES: A piece of the bones?

MASON: No, sir, not them. There's a central heating furnace under Lady Beatrice's room. It'd been off for some time, but Sir Robert started complaining of the cold, so it was started up again. Then the other morning, when one of the boys was raking out the cinders, he found this charred bone.

HOLMES: What do you make of this, Watson?

WATSON: It is the upper condyle of a human femur.

HOLMES: Exactly. Well, these are deep waters indeed. When did Sir Robert give away his sister's dog?

MASON: Just a week ago today. It was howling outside the old well-house and Sir Robert was in one of his tantrums that day. I thought he would have killed it, but he gave it to one of the jockeys and said to take it over to old Barnes at the Green Dragon. He said he never wanted to see it again.

HOLMES: Thank you. Now, who keeps Lady Beatrice Falder company most of the time?

MASON: Her maid, Carrie. She's been with her about five years. Her husband, Norlett, he's the footman.

HOLMES: Both no doubt devoted servants?

MASON: You need to be devoted to keep a job with Sir Robert. What he tells anyone to do, they do, and no questions.

HOLMES: Aha! Tell me, Mr. Mason, is there good fishing in that part of Berkshire?

MASON: Fishing, sir? Well, yes, there are trout in the mill-stream and pike in the Hall lake.

HOLMES: That's good enough. Dr. Watson and I are famous fishermen.

WATSON: Are we?

HOLMES: In fact, Mr. Mason, you may address us in future at the Green Dragon, Crendall. We should reach it tonight. I need hardly say that we do not wish to be seen with you down there, but a note will reach us if you want us.

SCENE FOUR

[*The bar of the Green Dragon, Crendall.* HOLMES *and* WATSON *are chatting with the landlord,* MR. BARNES]

HOLMES: Yes, thank you, Mr. Barnes, my friend and I are very comfortable indeed, very comfortable.

WATSON: Yes, very comfortable indeed.

HOLMES: Tell me, what do you think about the Hall lake and the chance of a pike?

BARNES: The Hall [*Laughs*] You might find yourselves *in* the lake before you were finished.

WATSON: I don't quite follow you.

BARNES: It's Sir Robert Norberton, sir. He's terrible jealous of touts.

WATSON: Touts!

BARNES: Beg pardon, sir, but if you two strangers were as near his training quarters as that he'd be after you, sure as fate.

HOLMES [*vaguely*]: I think I did hear that he has a horse entered for the Derby.

BARNES: He's carrying all our money and his own too. Begging your pardon, gentlemen – I suppose you *ain't* on the Turf yourselves?

WATSON: Certainly not!

HOLMES: No, indeed. Just two weary Londoners who badly need some good Berkshire air. Oh, by the way, Mr. Barnes, I wanted to ask you – what breed is that beautiful spaniel I saw in the passage just now?

BARNES: Ah, that's the real Shoscombe breed, sir. There's no better in England than that.

HOLMES: Really? What price would a dog like that cost?

BARNES: More than I could pay, sir. It was Sir Robert himself who gave me this one. He'd be off back to the Hall in a jiffy if I gave him his head. [*Going*] Now, if you'll excuse me, gentlemen?

WATSON: Well, Holmes?

HOLMES: I think, Watson, we might do well to enter the sacred domain tomorrow night, before Norberton returns.

WATSON: Have you any theory?

HOLMES: Only this. Something happened a week or two ago which has cut deep into the life of the Shoscombe household. What was it? We can only guess at it from its effects, and they seem to be of curiously mixed character. The brother no longer visits the beloved invalid sister.

He gives away her favourite dog. *Her* dog Watson. Does that suggest nothing to you?

WATSON: Nothing but the brother's spite.

HOLMES: Well, there is an alternative . . . But to continue our review of the situation: the lady keeps her room, alters her habits, is not seen save when she drives out with her maid, and refuses to stop at the stables even to greet her favourite horse. Let us suppose, therefore, that Sir Robert Norberton has done away with his sister . . .

WATSON: Holmes!

HOLMES: He's utterly in debt and may at any moment be sold up and his racing stables seized by his creditors. He is a daring and desperate man. He derives his income from his sister. His sister's maid and her husband are his willing tools.

WATSON: That's true.

HOLMES: But he could not fly the country until he had realized his fortune. And that fortune could only be realized by bringing off his win with Shoscombe Prince. Therefore, if he had disposed of his sister he would still have to stand his ground. He would have to get rid of her body in some way. With the servants as his confidantes, that would not be impossible. The body might be conveyed to the crypt, which is seldom visited, and it might later be secretly destroyed at night in the furnace, leaving behind it such evidence as we have seen. What say you to that, Watson?

WATSON: Monstrous!

HOLMES: Well, I think there is a small experiment which we may try tomorrow. In the meantime, if we mean to keep up our characters, I suggest we call for a glass of wine and hold some high converse upon eels and dace and that sort of thing.

SCENE FIVE

[*The same scene next morning*]

BARNES: Good morning, gentlemen, good morning. [*They greet him*] Why, I should have thought you'd have been away to your fishing long before this.

HOLMES: As a matter of fact, Mr. Barnes, my friend here rather foolishly forgot to pack our spoon-bait for jack, and as we gather there is none to be had hereabouts we shall just have to forget about the fish.

WATSON: It was only an excuse to get away from London, really, you know.

BARNES: Ah, well, there's some very nice walking in these parts.

HOLMES: As a matter of fact, I was just wondering to my friend whether you might be persuaded to let us take that dog of yours along with us?

BARNES: If you can be bothered with him, I reckon he'll be glad of the exercise. I don't seem to get ten minutes to call my own these days. I'll go and fetch him now.

SCENE SIX

[*The road outside the gates of Shoscombe Old Place.* HOLMES *has the dog on a lead*]

WATSON: This is Shoscombe Old Place, Holmes.

HOLMES: Doesn't the poor dog know it! Mm! I learn that

E

the old lady's carriage comes through here almost precisely every mid-day as she starts out for her drive.

WATSON: It's nearly mid-day now. Are you hoping for a glimpse of her?

HOLMES: More than that. The carriage has to slow down while the gates are being opened for it. Now when it comes through and before it gathers speed again, I want you to stop the coachman with some question.

WATSON: Oh well . . . very well.

HOLMES: As you do, I shall accidentally lose my hold on this good dog's lead. But quickly, Watson. I can see the carriage in the drive-way now. [*Going*] You know what to do?

WATSON: Yes! All right, Holmes.

> [*The carriage approaches, then slows and halts for the lodgekeeper to open the gates*]

LODGEKEEPER: Righto, mate!

> [*The carriage moves slowly through*]

WATSON: I say, pardon me . . . Coachman!

STEPHENS: Yes, sir?

WATSON: Can you tell me, is Sir Robert Norberton at home today?

STEPHENS: No, sir, he ain't back from London yet.

WATSON: Oh, I see . . .

> [HOLMES *has let the dog loose and it approaches with joyful cries, leaps up at the carriage door, then begins to snarl*]

STEPHENS: Get back with you. Get away or you'll get my whip!

> [*A high-pitched voice from inside the carriage cries:* 'Drive on! Drive on!']

> [*The carriage moves away. The dog whines pitifully*]

HOLMES [*approaching*]: Come here, boy, come here. You're too valuable to lose. Well, Watson, that's done it.

WATSON: It certainly caused enough excitement. Well, what did you see? There just seemed to be two of them in the carriage – the maid, perhaps, and the old lady. And yet . . .

HOLMES: Yes, Watson?

WATSON: Well, the dog. That snarling.

HOLMES: Exactly. He recognized his mistress's carriage, but found a stranger inside it. Dogs don't make mistakes. But did you notice anything else?

WATSON: I did think that voice – the one that called to him to drive on – it sounded more like a man's.

HOLMES: And we have added one more card to our hand. But it needs careful playing, all the same. I think we will arrange for another rendezvous this evening with our friend Mr. John Mason. And I think the Norberton crypt would be as good a place as any.

SCENE SEVEN

[*That night* HOLMES, WATSON *and* MASON *are in the crypt*]

MASON: I can't stay long, sir. The moment Sir Robert arrives home he'll want to see me to get the latest news of Shoscombe Prince.

HOLMES: In that case, Mr. Mason, you can just show us the bones you spoke of and leave us to it.

MASON: They're here in this corner. If you could shine your lantern, Dr. Watson . . .

WATSON: Here? There's nothing here.

MASON: Yes, sir . . . Why, they've gone!

HOLMES: As I expected. I fancy their ashes might even now be found in that furnace you told us about.

MASON: But why in the world would anyone want to burn the bones of someone who's been dead maybe hundreds of years?

HOLMES: That is what we are here to find out. It may mean a long search and we need not detain you.

MASON: Then I'll be off if you don't mind, sir. I don't want the master to find me missing.

[*He goes*]

HOLMES: Now, Watson, let us have a closer look at some of these tombs.

WATSON: What do you hope to find, Holmes?

HOLMES: Mm?

WATSON: I said what do you hope to find?

HOLMES: Ah! What have we here?

WATSON: A coffin, on its end. Made of lead from the look of it.

HOLMES: And, unless I am very much mistaken, recently tampered with. Just let me get my lens to it. Some light, please.

WATSON: Very well.

HOLMES: Hm! Yes! As I thought.

WATSON: Hm! Someone has tried to open it?

HOLMES: And succeeded, I should say. I think we shall now do the same, with the assistance of my trusty jemmy.

WATSON: Always prepared, Holmes.

HOLMES: One never knows.

[*He levers at the lid*]

Easy. Just a pull, Watson, if you please, and we have it.

[*With a final wrench and clatter the lid comes off*]

Now, then . . .

WATSON: Holmes! This is no ancient corpse. This is . . .

HOLMES: Listen!

WATSON: Someone's coming.

HOLMES: Too late to hide.

NORBERTON [*approaching*]: Who the devil may you be? And what are you doing on my property?

HOLMES: My name is Sherlock Holmes.

NORBERTON: Sherlock Holmes?

HOLMES: Possibly it is familiar to you. But in any case, my business is that of every other good citizen – to uphold the law. It seems to me that you have much to answer for, Sir Robert.

NORBERTON: Oh, it does, does it?

HOLMES: For instance, who was – or is – the occupant of this coffin?

NORBERTON [*a sigh*]: Very well, Mr. Holmes. Everything can be explained, I assure you. Appearances are against me, but everything is all right.

HOLMES: I am pleased to hear it.

NORBERTON: You have gone pretty deeply into my affairs Mr. Holmes, so you know in all probability that I am running a dark horse for the Derby and that everything depends on my success.

HOLMES: I understand the position.

NORBERTON: I am dependent upon my sister, Lady Beatrice, for everything. I have always known that if she were to die my creditors would be on to my estate like a flock of vultures. Everything would be seized – my stables, my horses, everything. Well, my sister *did die* – a week ago.

WATSON: And you told no one?

NORBERTON: How could I? If one word had got out, absolute ruin would have descended upon me within a matter of hours. If I could only stave things off for three weeks until the Derby – all would be well.

WATSON: *If* your horse wins.

NORBERTON: Well, if he doesn't . . .

WATSON: But in any case, surely your bets on the race and your expectations from it would hold good, even if your creditors did seize your estate?

NORBERTON: The horse would be part of my estate. And my chief creditor happens to be that same rascally fellow, Sam Brewer, whom I was once compelled to horsewhip on Newmarket Heath. If he got possession of the horse he would simply withdraw him from the race. My bets would be void and my ruin would be complete.

HOLMES: Sir Robert, of what did your sister die?

NORBERTON: Dropsy. It had plagued her for years.

HOLMES: Has a doctor certified to that effect?

NORBERTON: No. I catch your meaning. But I assure you, any doctor would certify that her end had been in no doubt for months now.

HOLMES: And it occurred just too soon for you. Well, what did you do?

NORLETT [*from above*]: Are you down there, sir?

NORBERTON: Yes. Come down, Norlett.

NORLETT [*approaching*]: Sir.

NORBERTON: Mr. Holmes, this is Norlett, the husband of my late sister's maid, Carrie. They are the two people upon earth who can substantiate what I say.

HOLMES: Very well.

NORBERTON: As I told you, I thought if I could only stave things off until after the Derby, all would be well. But obviously the body couldn't remain in the house, even though there was no need for anyone to enter her room but the maid. So on the first night Norlett and I carried it out to the old well-house.

NORLETT: I disclaim all responsibility.

NORBERTON: As I might expect. However, the responsibility is mine.

HOLMES: You concealed the body in the well-house.

NORBERTON: Yes. But then there was a complication over my sister's spaniel. It used to follow her everywhere. It turned up at the well-house door and stood there yapping continuously.

HOLMES: So you got rid of it to the landlord of the Green Dragon.

NORBERTON: Yes. Even so, I felt that some more secure place was needed for my sister's body, and Norlett and I carried it by night to the crypt. There was no indignity or irreverence, Mr. Holmes.

WATSON: Hm!

NORBERTON: It seemed to me it would be no unworthy resting-place if we put her for some time in one of the coffins of her late husband's ancestors. They lie in what is still consecrated ground. Norlett and I . . .

NORLETT: I disclaim . . .

NORBERTON: All right! We opened a coffin, removed the contents and placed my sister inside, as you have seen her. As to the old relics, they were burnt in the furnace at night. It seemed better than to leave them lying there for intruders to disturb.

HOLMES: After that it was but a case of arranging for someone to ride daily in your late sister's carriage, wearing her clothes, and keeping up the appearance that she was still alive and well.

NORBERTON: Just so.

HOLMES: I imagine, Mr. Norlett, you disclaim all responsibility in this as well?

NORLETT: I'd like to know who you think you . . .

NORBERTON: That will do, Norlett! You are quite right, Mr. Holmes. Norlett impersonated my sister and rode each day beside his wife, her maid.

HOLMES: Deceiving everyone except an unhappy dog who wondered where his mistress had got to.

NORBERTON: And you, it seems?

HOLMES: It is my business not to be deceived. It was my duty to bring the facts to light, and there I must leave it. As to the morality or decency of your own conduct, it is not for me to express any opinion.

SCENE EIGHT

[*The parlour of 221B some days later.* HOLMES *is busy with a microscope.* WATSON *enters with a newspaper*]

HOLMES: Ah, there you are, Watson. I thought I heard you go out a few minutes ago.

WATSON: Oh, ah, yes, I did. To buy a newspaper.

HOLMES: But our papers will be delivered before long, won't they?

WATSON [*chuckling*]: I know, Holmes. But I wanted one before.

HOLMES: Mm? Really, Watson, you have been uncommonly excited all afternoon, and now you are looking as smug as a well-filled cat. Pray, let me into your secret.

WATSON: Do you know what today is, Holmes?

HOLMES: Today? Christmas? Easter? St. Swithin's? No, I see nothing remarkable about it.

WATSON: This is Derby Day. The Derby was run this afternoon.

HOLMES: Oh, really? Is that all?

WATSON [*sighs*]: I should hesitate to bore you with the particulars. The Derby was won by a horse named Shoscombe Prince, of which you have doubtless heard. He carried with him the blessing of my month's wound pension. That is all.

HOLMES: Ah, the name *is* familiar. My dear Watson, do come and give me the benefit of your opinion upon this specimen. Really, if it were not for the microscope I do not believe we should achieve half the results we manage to...

WATSON: Oh, really, Holmes!

THE ILLUSTRIOUS CLIENT

Characters in order of appearance:

SHERLOCK HOLMES

DR. WATSON

SIR JAMES DAMERY: an elderly, respected figure in high circles.

BARON GRUNER: An Austrian-born adventurer in his late thirties or thereabouts.

SHINWELL JOHNSON: A reformed crook.

KITTY WINTER: A young woman of low class ruined by Baron Gruner.

NEWSPAPER BOY

THE ILLUSTRIOUS CLIENT

SCENE ONE

> [*The parlour of 221B Baker Street one morning.*
> WATSON *is examining an unopened letter, trying*
> *out his powers of deduction, watched by* HOLMES.

WATSON: Hm! Thumb-print in the top left-hand corner of the envelope. Postman's, probably.

> [*He takes the paper from the envelope and unfolds*
> *it*]

Addressed from the Carlton Club, yesterday evening, Holmes.

HOLMES [*yawning*]: Yes, Watson. Do go on!

WATSON: I was just about to. [*Reads*] 'Sir James Damery presents his compliments to Mr. Sherlock Holmes and will call upon him at 4.30 tomorrow. Sir James begs to say that the matter upon which he desires to consult Mr. Holmes is very delicate, and also very important.' Pretty formal, eh, Holmes?

HOLMES: Mm! What do you know of this man, Damery?

WATSON: Only that his name is a household word in Society.

HOLMES: I can tell you a little more than that. He has a reputation for arranging delicate matters which are to be kept out of the papers.

WATSON: Really?

HOLMES: He is a man of the world with a natural turn for diplomacy. I'm bound to hope, therefore, that this is not a false scent. He must have some real need of our assistance. And if I am not mistaken, that is his footstep upon our stair.

WATSON: Ah!

[*He opens the door*]

Sir James Damery?

DAMERY: That is so.

WATSON: Do come in, sir. This is Mr. Sherlock Holmes.

DAMERY: How do you do, Mr. Holmes? And Dr. Watson, I presume?

WATSON: Correct, sir.

DAMERY: Mr. Holmes may find your collaboration very necessary, I fancy.

HOLMES: Indeed? Pray take the basket chair, Sir James.

DAMERY: Thank you, Mr. Holmes.

HOLMES: Now, sir?

DAMERY: Mr. Holmes, we are dealing with a man to whom violence is familiar. I should say that there is no more dangerous man in Europe.

HOLMES: The *most* dangerous man in Europe? I have had several opponents to whom that flattering term has been applied.

DAMERY. Have you ever heard of Baron Gruner?

HOLMES: The Austrian murderer?

DAMERY: Oh! There's no getting past you at all, Mr. Holmes. So you've sized him up as a murderer already?

HOLMES: It is my business to follow the details of Continental crime. Who could possibly have read what happened at Prague and have any doubts about the man's guilt? It was a purely technical legal point and the death of a witness that saved him. I'm as sure he killed his wife when that so-called accident happened in the Splügen Pass as if I'd seen him do it.

DAMERY: Then you will sympathize with the client in whose interests I'm acting.

HOLMES: And who is your client, Sir James?

DAMERY: Mr. Holmes, I must beg you not to press that question. It is important that his honoured name should be in no way dragged into the matter.

HOLMES: I am sorry, Sir James. I am accustomed to mystery at one end of my cases, but to have it at both ends is too confusing.

DAMERY: Mr. Holmes, may I, at least, lay all that I can before you?

HOLMES: So long as it is understood that I commit myself to nothing.

DAMERY: You've no doubt heard of General de Merville?

WATSON: De Merville of the Khyber Pass?

DAMERY: The same.

HOLMES: Yes, I have heard of him.

DAMERY: He has a daughter, Violet. She is young, beautiful, accomplished – and very rich. It is this daughter, Mr. Holmes, whom we must save from the clutches of a fiend.

HOLMES: Baron Gruner has a hold over her?

DAMERY: The strongest of all holds where a woman is concerned – love. As you may have heard, the fellow is extraordinarily handsome, with a most fascinating manner and all that air of romance and mystery – well, you know what I mean – the sort of thing that means so much to a woman.

HOLMES: But how did he come to meet a lady of Miss Violet de Merville's standing?

DAMERY: It was on a Mediterranean yachting cruise. The villain attached himself to her and won her heart. She's obsessed by him. She won't hear a word against him. Everything has been done to cure her of it.

HOLMES: And so?

DAMERY: She proposes to marry him next month.

HOLMES: I see.

DAMERY: She has a will of iron, and she is of age.

HOLMES: Does she know about his past – the Austrian episode?

DAMERY: Ah, the cunning devil has told her every bit of scandal he's had a part in: but he's done it in such a way that he always turns out to be the innocent martyr.

WATSON: But surely, Sir James, in telling us all this you have inadvertently let out the name of your client?

DAMERY: General de Merville? Well, Dr. Watson, I could deceive you, perhaps, by letting you think that; but it wouldn't be true. De Merville is a broken old man. His daughter is set on marrying a scheming adventurer. All I dare say of my client is that he is an old friend who has known the General intimately for years, and cannot see this tragedy acted out without some attempt to stop it.

HOLMES: Sir James, your problem interests me. The Baron's present address, please?

DAMERY: Vernon Lodge, near Kingston. It's a large place. He's a rich man now, which I fancy makes him more dangerous than ever.

HOLMES: Can you give me anything further about him?

DAMERY: Well, expensive tastes, you know. Horse fancier, but quite an artistic side to him. I believe he's an authority on Chinese pottery. He wrote a book about it. Well, I'll say good day to you, gentlemen.

HOLMES: Good day.

WATSON: Good day, Sir James.

[*He exits*]

HOLMES: Well, Watson, any views?

WATSON: I suppose you will see the young lady yourself?

HOLMES: My dear Watson, if her poor old broken father can't move her, what can a stranger expect to do? No, I think we must begin from a different angle. Perhaps Shinwell Johnson could be a help.

WATSON: Shinwell Johnson! That ruffian!

HOLMES: He has the *entrée* to every night-club, doss-house and gambling den in this city. His two convictions have invested him with a certain glamour. He also has a quick eye and an active brain which, I am happy to say, have been placed at the disposal of the forces of law and order on more than one occasion. Repentance is a noble thing, Watson. Two terms in Parkhurst have worked wonders in Master Shinwell Johnson.

WATSON: An informer, eh?

HOLMES: Not really. If he'd acted for the police he'd have been found out by now. Fortunately, however, he confines his attention to cases which never come directly into the courts. I tell you what, Watson: we'll meet for dinner this evening at our place in the Strand, eh? Meanwhile, I'll just have a word or two with Master Shinwell Johnson – and another gentleman.

F

SCENE TWO

[HOLMES *and* WATSON *are eating at their restaurant in The Strand*]

HOLMES: Capital soup! Never varies, thank heaven.

WATSON: Never mind the soup, Holmes. You've a particularly nasty delight in keeping me waiting for your news.

HOLMES: There's nothing much to tell. Johnson is on the prowl for us. He may pick up some useful garbage in the darker recesses of the underworld.

WATSON: But surely, if the lady won't accept what's already known about Baron Gruner, why should anything we can find out change her mind for her?

HOLMES: Who knows? Who knows? Woman's heart and mind are insoluble puzzles to the male. Murder might be condoned or explained, and yet some smaller offence might rankle. As Baron Gruner remarked to me . . .

WATSON: Gruner remarked to you!

HOLMES: Oh, to be sure. You know how I love to come to grips with my man. I like to meet him, eye to eye, and read for myself what stuff he's made of. When I'd given Johnson his orders I took a cab out to Kingston. I found the Baron in a most affable mood.

WATSON: Did he recognize you?

HOLMES: Oh there was no difficulty about that. I sent in my card. He received me at once.

SCENE THREE

[*A 'flashback' to* HOLMES'S *interview with* BARON GRUNER *in the study of* GRUNER'S *house*]

GRUNER: I rather thought I should see you sooner or later, Mr. Holmes. You have been engaged, no doubt, by General de Merville, to try to stop my marriage with his daughter Violet? Is it not so?

HOLMES: As you wish.

GRUNER: My dear man, let me tell you at once, you will only ruin your well-deserved reputation – to say nothing of incurring some danger. Let me strongly advise you to draw off at once.

HOLMES: Curiously enough, that was the very advice I had intended giving you.

GRUNER: So?

HOLMES: I have a respect for your brains, Baron, and the little I've seen of your personality has not lessened it. But let me put it to you, as man to man.

GRUNER: Very well.

HOLMES: No one wants to rake up your past. It is over, and you are now in smooth waters. But if you persist in this adventurous marriage you will raise up a swarm of powerful enemies who will never leave you alone until they have made England too hot to hold you. I ask you, is the game worth it?

GRUNER [*he begins to chuckle, increasing to hearty laughter*] Oh, dear, excuse my amusement, Mr. Holmes. But it really is funny to see you trying to play a hand with no cards in it at all. I don't think anyone could do it better, but it is rather pathetic, all the same. Not a colour card there, Mr. Holmes: nothing but the smallest of the small.

HOLMES: If you choose to think so.

GRUNER: I know! Now let me make this thing clear to you, for my own hand is so strong I can afford to show it. I have been fortunate enough to win the entire affection of this lady. This has been given to me in spite of the fact that I told her clearly of all the *unhappy* incidents in my past life. I also told her that certain wicked and designing persons – I hope you recognize yourself – would come to her and tell her these things, and I warned her how to treat them.

HOLMES: Then there is nothing more to be said. [*Rising to go*] If you will excuse me, I will wish you good day, Baron Gruner.

GRUNER: Certainly. The pleasure has all been mine. But, before you go, though, Mr. Holmes . . .

HOLMES: Well?

GRUNER: Did you know Le Brun, the French agent?

HOLMES [*returning*]: Yes, I knew him.

GRUNER: Do you know what happened to him?

HOLMES: I heard he was beaten by some Apaches in Montmartre and crippled for life.

GRUNER: Quite true. By a curious coincidence, though, he had been inquiring into my affairs only a week before. Don't do it, Mr. Holmes; it's not a lucky thing to do.

SCENE FOUR

[*We return to* HOLMES *and* WATSON *at the restaurant table*]

HOLMES: So, there you are, Watson. You are up to date at last.

WATSON: The fellow seems dangerous enough.

HOLMES: Mighty dangerous. I disregard the blusterer, but this is the sort of man who says rather less than he means.

WATSON: Must you interfere? I mean, does it matter so much if he does marry the girl? They're free to choose, after all.

HOLMES: Considering that he undoubtedly murdered his last wife, I should say it mattered very much. Our illustrious client evidently thinks so too. But come along, drink up your coffee and come home with me. Our friend Shinwell Johnson is due to call on us.

SCENE FIVE

[*The parlour of 221B.* SHINWELL JOHNSON *and* KITTY WINTER *are just entering*]

HOLMES: Come in, Johnson, come in.

JOHNSON: Gentlemen, allow me to introduce Miss Kitty Winter, who I took the liberty of bringing along of me. What she don't know . . . ah, but she can speak for 'erself.

KITTY: Yes, we're old mates, Shinwell and me, mister. Same address, almost, eh? Hell, London, that's it. Finds us every time. But there's a chap who ought to be down in a lower hell than us if there was any justice in the world, I tell you.

HOLMES: I gather we have your good wishes in our little investigation, Miss Winter?

KITTY: I'll say so! If I can 'elp put Adelbert Gruner where 'e belongs, I'm yours to the rattle.

WATSON: You know him, then?

KITTY: What I am, Gruner made me, straight 'e did.

HOLMES: Has Shinwell told you how the matter stands?

JOHNSON: I 'ave, sir. Left nothin' out.

HOLMES: The lady is madly in love with him, Miss Winter. She's been told everything about him, but she cares nothing.

KITTY: Told about the murder of his wife?

HOLMES: Yes.

KITTY: She must 'ave a nerve.

HOLMES: She puts it all down as lies.

KITTY: Can't you show 'er proofs?

HOLMES: What proofs?

KITTY: Well – well, ain't I a proof meself? If I went and told 'er 'ow 'e used me . . .

WATSON: Would you do that?

KITTY: Would I! There's one or two more murders than the one what made such a fuss. I know a few things. An' there's that book of 'is . . .

HOLMES: A book?

KITTY: I tell you, mister, that man collects women like anyone collects butterflies or moths. They're all in that book – all the details.

WATSON: Shameful!

KITTY: Names, snapshots, things you wouldn't believe any man would write down. That'd show 'er a thing or two. An' I know where 'e keeps it.

WATSON: You do?

KITTY: Well, leastways, I know where 'e always *did* keep it. Special place, 'e 'ad, in a big cabinet thing. Where 'e keeps a lot of 'is Chinese crockery.

HOLMES: Very interesting, Miss Winter. I think I shall take advantage of your offer to confront the lady in question with what you know. As for the book, I think we will keep that to ourselves for the time being. Then, if all else fails . . . Watson . . .

WATSON: Yes, Holmes?

HOLMES: Tomorrow morning, Miss Winter and I will pay our call. Be good enough to meet me for luncheon afterwards, and I'll post you up. Our place in the Strand will do, I think.

WATSON: Very well, Holmes.

SCENE SIX

> [WATSON *is approaching the restaurant in the Strand when he hears a* NEWSPAPER BOY *approaching*]

NEWSVENDOR: Paper! Paper! Murderous attack on famous detective! Paper! Sherlock Holmes attacked in Regent Street. Paper!

WATSON: What's that? Here, my boy!

NEWSVENDOR: Here y'are, guv'nor.

WATSON [*impatiently*]: All right, keep the change.

NEWSVENDOR: Ta very much, guv'. [*Going*] Paper, paper! Murderous attack on famous detective . . .

WATSON: Great heavens! [*Reads quickly to himself*] 'Mr. Sherlock Holmes, the well-known detective, victim, murderous assault. Attacked about twelve o'clock. Regent Street, two men with sticks, beaten about the head, injuries, doctors describe as serious, taken Charing Cross Hospital, afterwards insisted taken to his own rooms . . .' [*Shouts*] Here, cabby, cabby!

[*A hansom cab drives up*]

Quick as you can go, man: 221B Baker Street. Go for your life!

[*The cab drives him away quickly*]

SCENE SEVEN

[HOLMES, *pale and bandaged, is reclining on the settee in the parlour of 221B*]

HOLMES [*weakly*]: All right, Watson, my dear fellow. Don't look so scared. It's not as bad as it seems.

WATSON: Thank heaven for that!

HOLMES: I'm not so bad at single-stick myself. Took most of their blows on my guard. It was the second fellow that was too much for me.

WATSON: The papers say they got away.

HOLMES: They were well prepared.

WATSON: Shall I go to the police?

HOLMES: No, wait a little. I have my plans. The first thing is to exaggerate my injuries.

WATSON: Who to?

HOLMES: Everyone. They'll come to you for news. Lay it on thick – lucky if I live the week out; concussion; delirium. You can't overdo it.

WATSON: Very well. Anything else?

HOLMES: Tell Shinwell Johnson to get that girl, Kitty Winter, out of the way. If they dared try to do me in it's not likely they'll neglect her.

WATSON: I'll go now.

HOLMES: Right. Oh, and put out my pipe on the table, will you, and the tobacco. Come in each morning, and we'll plan our campaign.

SCENE EIGHT

[*The same scene, the following day.* HOLMES *is clearly much better*]

WATSON: Well, Holmes, you are looking better. [*Chuckle*] Tonight's papers say you've developed erysipelas.

HOLMES: Capital, my dear fellow! I shall enjoy having that very much.

WATSON: Seriously though, Holmes, I've some news you won't find so amusing.

HOLMES: What?

WATSON: Baron Gruner sails from Liverpool on Friday.

HOLMES: Sails?

WATSON: To the States. Important business to settle before his impending marriage, etcetera, etcetera.

HOLMES: Friday! Only three more days. Mark my words, he wants to put himself out of harm's way until the last moment. But he won't, Watson. By the Lord Harry, he won't! Now, listen. I want you to do something for me.

WATSON: Of course, Holmes.

HOLMES: Spend the next twenty-four hours studying Chinese pottery.

WATSON: Very well . . . Studying Chinese pottery!

HOLMES: Your friend Lomax at the London Library should be just the man to help. Now, now, no questions: off you go to your crammer. I'll see you here tomorrow evening.

SCENE NINE

[*The same scene next day.* HOLMES *is fully recovered*]

WATSON: Well, Holmes, I shall never be able to believe the newspapers again after this. They say you're dying.

HOLMES: Well done, Watson. No, as you see, I'm on my legs again and feeling none the worse. And now, have you learned your lessons?

WATSON: As best I could. It's a big subject.

HOLMES: Chinese ceramics in twenty-fours: granted, granted. The point is, could you keep up an intelligent conversation on the subject?

WATSON: I think so. For a while, anyway.

HOLMES: Then, pray, hand me that little box. Thank you. Now, take a look at this.

WATSON: I say!

HOLMES: This saucer is the real egg-shell pottery of the Ming Dynasty.

WATSON: Exquisite!

HOLMES: The sight of this would drive a real connoisseur wild. You'll have to handle it carefully.

WATSON: *I* shall?

HOLMES: I should say, Dr. Hill Barton, of No. 369 Half Moon Street, must handle it carefully. That is your name for this evening, Watson. And here is a visiting card I've had prepared for you.

WATSON: And what is Dr. Hill Barton to do?

HOLMES: At half-past eight he will call upon Baron Gruner. An appointment has been made, saying you are bringing with you a specimen of an absolutely unique set of Ming. You are a collector. This piece has come your way. You have heard of the Baron's interest in the subject, and you're not averse to selling, at a price.

WATSON: What price?

HOLMES: Well asked, Watson. You would certainly fall down badly if you didn't know the value of your own wares. Actually, this saucer was got for me by Sir James Damery. You will not be exaggerating if you suggest that it could hardly be matched in the world today.

WATSON: Then I could suggest that the set could be valued by an expert.

HOLMES: Excellent!

WATSON: And having done all that . . . ?

HOLMES: No more instructions, my dear chap. We will let the interview take care of itself.

SCENE TEN

[BARON GRUNER's *study that evening*]

GRUNER: Pray, sit down, Dr. Barton. I was just looking over my own treasures and wondering whether I could really afford to add to them. This little Tang specimen from the seventh century will interest you, I am sure?

WATSON: Ah, yes. Delightful.

GRUNER: Did you ever see finer workmanship, or a better glaze?

WATSON: No!

GRUNER: But have you the Ming saucer with you?

WATSON: Here it is, Baron Gruner. What do you think of that?

GRUNER: Ah! Very fine – very fine indeed. And you say you have a set of six to correspond?

WATSON: That is so.

GRUNER: What puzzles me is that I should not have heard of such magnificent specimens. I only know one in England to match this, and it is certainly not likely to be on the market. Would it, er, be indiscreet, Doctor, to ask how you obtained this?

WATSON: Does it really matter? You can see it is genuine for yourself. As to the value, I am content to take an expert's valuation.

GRUNER: That the piece is genuine is certain. And yet, in dealing with objects of such value one naturally wishes to know all about the transaction. Suppose it should prove afterwards that you had no right to sell?

WATSON: I would guarantee you against any claim of that sort.

GRUNER: That, of course, would open up the question as to what your guarantee was worth.

WATSON: My bankers would answer that.

GRUNER: Quite so. Quite so. And yet the whole transaction strikes me as rather unusual.

WATSON: Well, Baron, I should hate to waste your valuable time. [*Rising*] I have given you first offer, as I understood you were a connoisseur, but I shall have no difficulty in other quarters.

GRUNER: No. May I ask, Doctor, who told you I was a connoisseur?

WATSON: You have written a book on the subject.

GRUNER [*quickly*]: Have you read the book?

WATSON: Er, no.

GRUNER: Dear me, this becomes more and more difficult to understand. You, too, are a connoisseur and collector, with a piece as valuable as this in your hands, and yet you have never troubled to consult the one book which would have told you its value!

WATSON: I'm a very busy man. I am a doctor in practice.

GRUNER: If a man has a hobby, he follows it up, whatever his other pursuits may be. Well, as a connoisseur, you would have no objection if I asked you a few questions to test you? [*Quickly and with mounting force*] I would ask you, what do you know of the Emperor Shomu and how do you associate him with the Shoso-in, near Nara? Tell me a little about the northern Wei dynasty and its place in the history of ceramics?

WATSON [*rising quickly*]: Really, sir, this is intolerable!

GRUNER: Do you even know how many Ming Dynasties there were?

WATSON: Sir, I came here to do you a favour, and not be examined like a schoolboy. My knowledge may be inferior to yours, but I shall certainly not answer questions put in so offensive a way!

GRUNER: No, Dr. Barton – if you are a doctor at all.

WATSON: How dare you cast aspersions . . . !

GRUNER: You are here on another game. You're an emissary of Sherlock Holmes, aren't you? The fellow's dying, so he sends his hirelings to keep watch on me. Isn't that it? Well, you've made your way in here, and by heaven, you may find it harder to get out again.

[*The french window crashes open.* HOLMES *enters*]

HOLMES [*off*]: All right, Watson: now you can leave it to me.

GRUNER: What's this!

[*He jerks open a drawer in his desk*]

WATSON: Careful, Holmes. He's getting a gun!

[KITTY WINTER *enters by the french window and pushes her way past* HOLMES *and* WATSON. *She is carrying a small bottle*]

KITTY: Out of my way, everyone. It's my turn now.

WATSON: Miss Winter!

HOLMES: Keep back!

KITTY: Oh no, this won't take a second. There, Baron Adelbert Gruner!

[*She dashes the contents of the bottle into* GRUNER'S *face*]

GRUNER [*screams*].

KITTY: That face won't charm any more like me again!

[GRUNER *staggers about, clutching his face*]

WATSON: Vitriol, all over his face. Quick, Holmes, for the love of heaven find me some kind of oil. We may save his eyes if we're quick enough. But hurry, hurry!

SCENE ELEVEN

[*Later that evening, back at 221B*. SIR JAMES
DAMERY *is with* HOLMES *and* WATSON]

WATSON: Horrible, Holmes: horrible!

HOLMES: The wages of sin, Watson – the wages of sin. And believe me, there was plenty of sin to answer for.

WATSON: But not like that.

HOLMES: I assure you, Watson, I had no idea she had vitriol with her. She came with me to find that book she told us about. Our time was limited by your knowledge of Chinese ceramics. It was our last chance, you understand, Sir James.

DAMERY: Of course, of course. The man was a murderer, Watson, and would have been again.

WATSON: Well, I suppose so. Anyway, he's disfigured for life, now. Miss Violet de Merville is out of danger.

DAMERY: So it seems.

HOLMES: Not yet, I'm afraid. Women of her type don't react like that. She would probably love him all the more as a disfigured martyr. No, Sir James: take this filthy book back to your client and tell him not to spare her feelings with it. It is his moral side that has to be destroyed, not the physical. This book will bring her down to earth as nothing else could. It is in his own writing. She can't get past that.

DAMERY: Very well. It's been a terrible business, but you've done wonders, both of you. [*Going*] Good day.

WATSON ⎱
HOLMES ⎰ : Good day, Sir James.

[*He exits*]

HOLMES: The police will have a good deal to say to Miss Kitty Winter, I fear, Watson. Though in her case there are certainly extenuating circumstances.

WATSON: I expect you're right. But to think that any woman . . .

[*He wanders away towards the window*]

HOLMES: Ah, me, I fear you have something to learn yet. If I were to tell you . . .

WATSON: Holmes, quickly! Come to the window.

HOLMES: Why, what is it?

WATSON: Sir James Damery. That brougham he just got into. See it? There. Moving off now. The coat of arms on the side.

HOLMES: Aha!

WATSON: Now I know who our illustrious client was. He's . . .

HOLMES: He's a chivalrous gentleman and a loyal friend to a lady in great danger. Let that be enough for us, my dear Watson, now and for ever.